MW01633582

HOLE IN THE HEAD: A LIFE REVEALED

A TRUE STORY

To Shannya.
Best Always.

2015

WILBERT L. SMITH PH.D.

ISBN-13: 978-1-934556-41-2
Library of Congress Control Number: 2011913780

Editor: Erica Mongé-Greer
Layout & Design: TABIA GRAPHICS & Bonita Jewel
Cover Design: Michael Walberg
Photos: Wilbert L. Smith and James "Buddy" Fowler
Period Photos: Lyles Station Consolidated School Museum
Pages of a book curved: © Refat Mamutov | Dreamstime.com

Printed in the United States of America

WILBERT SMITH Ph.D.

Wilbert Smith is an author and award winning filmmaker who strives to captures the essence and power of the human spirit. An outgoing and articulate personality, Wilbert holds a Master of Arts Degree in Special Education and a Ph.D. in Business Management.

"I have had an opportunity to do a number of wonderful things in my life. If I had to pick those that meant the most, they would be the activities that allowed the greatest impact on the lives of young people–the election to my local school board, and my appointment as Director of Child Development Programs by the governor of California,"

Wilbert also served as a prestigious member of California's Community Colleges Board of Governors, contributing to the establishment of policy and procedure for the state's more than one hundred community colleges. He has also taught in the School of Business at Pasadena Community College where he educated and inspired others with messages of knowledge and hard work.

When not writing, filmmaking or adding guidance to the lives of others, Wilbert owns and operates an insurance agency in Altadena, Ca. Where he specializes in all lines of insurance.

www.uplitproductionsinc.com

Acknowledgements

First I give honor to God and thank Him for those who entered my life as channels of support during the completion of this work. I also gratefully acknowledge the following individuals:

My wife Susan and children Kellie, Brian and Brandon Smith, who provided unconditional love and understanding during the completion of this work.

Brett Leonard, director of the documentary, Hole In The Head: A Life Revealed, for his encouragement and contribution to this story.

Bruce Byers, Elbert Payton and Mary Madison, who consistently honored my request for research and information.

Juliana Jones, Mother Love, Antonio Martin, Howard Siegel and Steven Sorrell for their constructive evaluation and Develyn Biagas who assisted with story editing.

The pastors and members of Bethel, Deliverance Tabernacle, Friendship, Metropolitan, Morning Star, New Macedonia and New Revelation for their dedication and support.

Thank you from the bottom of my heart for your faith, love and encouragement.

Dedication

This book is dedicated to my family members without whose sacrifice and assistance this book would not have been possible. And to my staff members who ran the extra mile in freeing up my time for travel and research in order to make this book possible. Finally, I offer sincere appreciation to the men and women of Lyles Station Indiana who dedicated time and effort for this project.

I hope this book brings appreciation and thankfulness for each day given and for those yet to be lived. Through the profound message of patience and understanding, perhaps readers will develop appreciation for tolerance and forgiveness, while they witness one man's shining example.

This story might fill a societal void that should be embraced by all who pause from life's rollercoaster-like rhythm long enough to cultivate an appreciation of life's infinite beauty and resources, receiving the very best that life has to offer. Reading this story might even be the single most important action, to potentially satisfy our innermost quest to change the world.

Contents

FOREWORD

Hole In The Head: A Life Revealed aptly describes the outcome of an inhumane act against ten young children, recounting vivid descriptions of the heavy burden Vertus Hardiman endured for 80 years.

Yes—this one event shaped his lifestyle, but nothing could alter his character. As a result of this experience, Vertus Hardiman became a virtual soloist that moved through life alone. All the while, he was protecting a secret in ways that made it obvious something was amiss. For most people, he was simply a bit unusual. Not many took the time to inquire about his curious hairstyle or head coverings, even on the hottest of days when others were shedding "all" in the interest of cooling off.

Mr. Hardiman proudly wore the title of custodian and janitor, which today, for most of the world translates into sanitation engineer. He made the most of the earnings gained in that profession. This humble man allowed himself to be used as a vessel of love that permeated throughout his life.

Then, when he allowed his story to be told—a story of being victimized in the name of scientific advances and innovative medical treatment, Vertus Hardiman revealed how he had moved on without thoughts of malice or revenge. From this example, we can only be left with the clear notion that he preached the greatest sermon a human being could, simply by living a life that embodied love. He did not always utter the words, nor make proclamations. Mr. Hardiman just lived his sermon by practicing forgiveness. Now, his loving spirit enriches us, as we apply the principles lived by him into our lives.

The messages of:

- Self – sharing how he was led to forgive.
- Treasures – unselfishly modeling the endowment of his life's work to charity.
- Talent – joining in to sing praises in spite of his sufferings.
- Time – leaving a legacy that will instruct and inform generations to come.

I am so glad that Vertus Hardiman's life touched mine. First, when I served as the Presiding Elder in the jurisdiction that included the church where he worshipped, and where for a short interim I served as Pastor of that congregation. Little did I realize the enormity of his spirit, nor the depth of his faith; but now, I can attest that he will live on in the lives of all mankind.

We can be thankful that Mr. Hardiman came our way and that he has shared his journey through the transmission of his struggles and triumphs in the volume *Hole In the Head: A Life Revealed.* It is my hope that readers of this story will seek a true understanding of his journey and be cleansed of any hatred of wrongdoers, and be able to proclaim how much love has consumed our lives.

Let us look at the world as Vertus did for, "When you change the way you look at things, then the things you look at change." Vertus Hardiman, thank you for modeling a remarkable walk. We pledge to go and do likewise!

Bishop Carolyn Tyler Guidry
Presiding Bishop – African Methodist Episcopal Church
Chairperson –Social Action Commission

PROLOGUE

In this book, I introduce to you Vertus Hardiman, a man who survived life on his own terms in spite of experiencing a tragic childhood event with all the earmarks of a Dr. Frankenstein film via an improper medical experiment, conducted in an Indiana hospital in Vertus' hometown. Vertus was five years old when he was removed for medical tests on his first day of school. The documented target was scalpel ringworm, a disease that lured nine boys and one girl towards treatment. In the end, it was discovered only to be a web spun by greed and the pursuit of power as perpetrators forced innocent children into test tubes as centerpieces for a malicious experiment. Unsuspecting parents were helpless. For Vertus, the resulting humility created an unthinkable defect that he hid under a wig for 80 years. For most of Vertus' life, his wig became his true companion and confidant.

This is also the story of a remarkable friendship that grew between Vertus and myself, as he became a role model and father figure. Through his friendship, I gained wisdom, learned about forgiveness and formed virtue of character that helped me to appreciate every day I am alive. What became most valuable though was the opportunity to enter into a journey of research that led to a compelling story. This book is its full telling.

Vertus' story is both inspiring and uplifting. Vertus the child grew to be a man who taught those around him invaluable lessons of love and compassion. In spite of his own life challenges, he lived abundantly. Not a day went by that escaped his memory of the horrific childhood violation, but Vertus remained ardent in the present. When asked the obvious question, "Are you angry or bitter?" Vertus always replied, "No, why should I be?" Vertus' interpretation has made me a better person. It is through his story that my life was impacted in such a way that enabled me to turn from a course of misdirection and receive the goodness life has to offer.

It is my hope that while reading this book you are transformed and inspired to believe. It was once said that being around Vertus is not an introduction, but an experience. I welcome you to journey through these pages and experience the story of a man who was dealt a harsh blow in life, yet chose to live with a triumphant human spirit.

To My Left

This story begins for me in 1986 when I visited First A.M.E. (FAME) Church in Pasadena, California. Theirs was a progressive ministry, known for its cultural diversity and talented music ministry. On any given Sunday, it wasn't unusual to find the city's finest musicians, singers and composers united, especially during holiday seasons. Choir members dedicated large amounts of time to prepare pageants for the enjoyment of local community.

Attending my first rehearsal, a particular man stood to my left. He was slim and short statured. He wore horn-rimmed glasses as thick as coke bottles on his face and embraced you with his smile, and he introduced himself to me almost immediately. "Hi, I'm Vertus Hardiman." We shook hands and he joked that he was a 63-year-old choir member that had been a standing member of that same choir for 64 years.

Vertus appeared to be quite a gentleman, standing approximately 5'6" and weighing about 145 pounds. He wore a bright red shirt and matching colorful tie to compliment his suit; I assumed he was a businessman. He smiled a lot and after hearing someone refer to me as Dr. Wilbert Smith, he leaned close to me and said, "That's wonderful, I like that Dr. Smith." I smiled my approval at him, genuinely uplifted by his positive demeanor.

There was something strange about Vertus. It wasn't his height, nor was it strange that he looked years younger than his actual age of sixty-four. What I found most odd had everything to do with his hairstyle. He wore a wig that was coal black. It covered his head from hairline to hairline. The style reminded me of an old-fashioned grease slicked shiny wig worn by an Elvis Presley impersonator. It was tall on the top and slender on the sides and looked as though at any given moment he was ready to burst out with the song *Blue Suede Shoes.*

I was amused, at first. Though Vertus was an older man, the wig didn't house a single strand of gray hair. There was no question about whether or not Vertus wore a wig. It was a one hundred percent certainty. After meeting him, I found myself internalizing questions like, "Doesn't Vertus realize just how unnatural he looks?" A natural looking wig would perhaps improve his overall look. But, I came to regret my early criticism when I uncovered the truth about this specific wig.

Since I had arrived at rehearsal early, I sat back and watched this gentleman. I couldn't help myself. Everyone was drawn to him. "Well, good evening Mr. Hardiman," the young, old and somewhere in between would say. "Hello, ev-very-bod-ee" he would respond, with the same bright smile and a handshake." He went out of his way to acknowledge and show respect to everyone around him.

I watched him open a choir entrance door for some younger ladies. He stopped a mother with a small child to hug and greet them. He told the child, "Now, remember the rules at church. I'll give you a lollipop if you sit quietly." The young girl raised her head and accepted the candy, along with the offer. I heard him speak with countless others replying to their courtesies, "I am great thank you." Vertus was extremely polite, responding always with "Yes, please," or "Thank you" for every gesture.

I quickly learned that in this church, Vertus was a celebrity. As soon as the choir director entered the room, she walked directly over to me—"Thank you, Dr. Smith, for lending your abilities to us. By the way, have you met our senior member, Mr. Hardiman?" When I shared with her our introduction, she was not surprised that we had already engaged in conversation previous to the introduction. Vertus' friendly nature was well known.

She directed me to sing next to Vertus. After five minutes of warm up vocals, I noticed that he was singing off pitch. I concluded he did not have strong vocal excellence and wondered if my new assignment was to correct him. Well, from that first night, when he was searching for his note, I turned in his direction and sang directly into his ear to get him into musical pitch.

Vertus wasn't shy in the least. He sang just as loud and enthusiastically as anyone else and he did it with a smile. No matter that I was there attempting to prompt his singing, most times it didn't seem to make a difference and he seldom recognized when he was off. It was as if he was a one-man show and his off key harmonies were a part of the comedy. In this way, though, we grew accustomed to each other's musical style.

Vertus was also challenged by the side-to-side sway used by most gospel choirs, perhaps a rhythmic lacking, as best I could explain. After years of trying to correct him, the choir director just accepted his lack of rhythm and let him do his own thing. After all, he had been in the choir for as long as many of them had been alive. The choir was his passion and off pitched harmony or lack of rhythm did not bother him at all.

In time, I learned how he came to this church and became involved. He had been a member since the early fifties and served as choir treasurer and librarian. As a rule, choir members arrived early each Sunday morning to receive last minute instruction from the director. Because of his friendliness, Vertus and I would talk and get to know each other during this preparation time. I listened carefully and was interested in what he had to say. I was building a friendship with him.

One of the first of many meaningful nuggets he offered had to do with his perception of how people over-decorated themselves with clothing, jewelry and the like compared to the meager investment they made to develop their heart, mind and soul. He said, "We decorate withering bodies when we need to be most concerned with our soul." I was intrigued and began to enjoy listening and learning from his old and tested wisdom.

Several Sundays passed while Vertus and I got to know each other, chatting after church. I realized that he was becoming a dear friend, someone who I looked forward to seeing and joking with. It turns out that we had a lot in common. For instance, I learned that we were both businessmen, both owned real estate and believed in saving through investments. During one conversation, he shared that he grew up from humble beginnings and never forgot the harsh lessons taught him during his childhood.

One Sunday I invited him out to brunch after service. I asked if he wanted to go to Sizzler or a fancier restaurant. He insisted on going to Denny's, where he said the prices were more reasonable. Once there, he would search the menu closely for "Senior Specials." This is where I really began to see for myself his beliefs about saving and avoiding wasteful spending.

At times, it would take him close to twenty minutes to order the same menu item because he had to look carefully at the complete menu for new selections or ways to order each item separately for a cheaper price. I used to joke and ask him to order before the restaurant closed. He would answer back, "Nope, not this one. It's a 24 hour restaurant."

During these brunch meals, he began to impart wisdom that became life lessons that I adopted. He encouraged me to spend wisely giving as the example his shopping regularly at thrift stores. He said, "You can find shirts, slacks, suits and ties" and would boast about the bargain prices paid. His favorite store was located just two blocks from his home. He joked that the store employees knew his interest well and called him in advance to offer his favorite item(s).

After our meetings, I watched him drive off in a 1986 Mustang. When I asked him about his older model car, he boasted "It has over two hundred thousand miles on its odometer". He said it was in good condition except for one flaw; when the air conditioner was activated, it caused the engine to overheat. Instead of repairing the problem, Vertus relied on outside air, rolling down the window for comfort. Plus I think he enjoyed the ability to slow down and wave and chat with neighbors and fellow members of this small community.

He later told me "I am not concerned about the age of a car as long as it gets me to the bowling alley, a bridge game, Denny's and church." As long as it got him where he wanted to go, Vertus was satisfied. He later told me, "You know Dr. Smith, I'd prefer to help somebody else before wasting money on myself."

And that's exactly what he did. I watched him give quarters to the young people for every "A" grade recorded on their report card. He donated money for church charities and helped in preparation and serving of meals. If he found out that a church member needed an item that he possessed, he would just give it to them. He donated many things to appreciative church members or tenants. As those that knew him would say, "That is just Vertus." And that was precisely the Vertus I was getting to know.

"You'd be surprised just how much you can achieve when you save and don't waste your money."

- Vertus

Always Welcome

I remember my first visit to his condominium. Vertus asked me to stop and talk about the prospect of doing business together. Vertus stated that he trusted me and knew that I would competently manage his accounts. His home was immaculate, filled with vintage furniture handed down through generations. When I first saw the old furniture I was reminded of my boyhood days of the mid 1950s when these styles were popular.

In his bedroom was a cherry wood bedroom set once belonging to his parents. His dining area housed an old red colored 1950s styled chrome legged table and chairs. His living room was furnished with antique French provincial furniture. The sofa was a shade of pink and looked to be in excellent condition. "Vertus," I said, "You have some antique gems here. Surely there's a fortune." He replied to me, "Dr. Smith, I bet you know me by now—all of this means little; I've just kept what I was given."

I noticed his condo was not very large at all. His kitchen for instance was very plain. I saw no microwave to heat or cook in and his stove was decades old, containing no clock, timer or fancy gadgetry. He had just enough to get by. I learned later why this was.

I also saw little evidence of family and asked if he had ever been married. Vertus looked downward and it was my first hint of what ticked inside. I could hear his loneliness, as he stated, "No, I never married, had any children or much family in California." He added, "Well, Dr. Smith, sometimes things happen to you that change the way you interact with others." I thought he was talking about the Great Depression or some other shared tragedy. At this time, I had no idea what had impacted him, bearing upon his choice to live alone all his life. I would not understand the whole picture until much later.

We sat for hours as I learned about his philosophy on living and investing. Vertus gave me specific lessons he learned during the Depression. He stated, "There were no food stamps, unemployment insurance or any other form of government assistance." Vertus described families who like the Hardimans suffered when fathers, the only workers in the household lost their jobs. "When I was a kid we had no shoes to wear and our clothes were hand-me-downs. We had little food to eat. Then came the Great Depression, and things got even tougher."

Vertus had two uncles who had saved several thousand dollars, which vanished with the collapse of banks. This directly impacted their future, vanquishing a year's worth of farming wages and seed money earmarked for planting the next year's harvest. Vertus recalled the negative impact this made. He would never trust in banks or allow them to take custody of his finances. Vertus didn't even own a checking account, choosing cash and an occasional money order to conduct his business.

We traveled down memory lane that evening holding conversations about his younger years and the lessons he learned from adolescence. He told me about the joy he felt with earning a high school diploma but said nothing about ever attending college. I assumed it had something to do with racial unrest, but as this story continues, you will learn why my assumptions were wrong.

He talked about life after high school. He said, "Following high school I got a day job with the County of Los Angeles. Each evening I also worked at a Catholic school. I was a janitor at both locations daily, one job full-time and the other part-time." While working for the county, he worked his way up to the rank of department head. I would eventually learn from one of his past employees about Vertus' dedication to encouraging those who worked beneath him, even those who worked in the lowliest jobs, to apply for promotions.

He proudly shared the story of his first home purchase, although I later learned it was just one of many. In 1951, Vertus purchased this home for five thousand dollars, in cash. To earn the purchase money, he worked two jobs and saved every possible dollar to meet his goal. Once he had earned enough money, he purchased the house without a loan. This was an honorable achievement. When I spoke about his strong work ethic he answered, "Look, I figured I could rest when I'm dead."

As we enjoyed each other's company that evening, we wrapped up by discussing topics such as landlording and finance, family and the good old days. I remember him continually saying, "My philosophy is, if I am greedy, I will lose. I'm not gonna spend every day of my remaining life holding onto something I can't take with me when I die."

We lost track of the original reason I came to visit, which pertained to the insurance policies for his properties. The paperwork was left, spread out over the dining room table. We decided he would drop by the office the next day and we could handle the business then. Before I left, I told Vertus how happy I was to have visited and reminded him that he was such a good businessman and great role model. At the time I didn't realize just how much this conversation, and others yet to come, would impact my future.

"My father was a serious man who taught that in order to have anything worthwhile, it would require you working extra hard to achieve it."

-Vertus

JUST STOPPING BY

As promised, Vertus stopped by my office. This became a weekly habit. Our relationship grew into one of accountability as we came together to discuss our business, including both insurance and rental property management.

On his first visit I introduced him to each employee, telling everyone that he was a person to get to know and emulate. But Vertus' personality and kind gestures spoke for themselves. He smiled wide and warm, while greeting each employee. He gave compliments while looking to find something praiseworthy about each person in the office, including customers being serviced. He asked, "And who is this handsome young man, or lovely lady," when being introduced to someone new. He then would reach into his pocket and hand them his traditional treat, a Tootsie Roll lollipop. The staff grew to love Vertus' cheerful spirit, and over the years they anticipated his weekly visits.

Vertus circulated around our small community, well liked and respected. Our business together also grew during this time; I eventually insured twenty-eight properties for him. One could not help but admire his success, especially considering the inconspicuous way he carried himself leading one to conclude that he was a person of few resources. He never wore diamonds or expensive clothing and didn't drive an expensive car. I never saw him showcase his money or brag about successful business investments or possessions. However, I learned later he was worth millions.

One night after visiting with Vertus, I told my wife about some of his many accomplishments. I shared with her my curiosity with his wig and how I wished I could refer him to a family friend who was a hair stylist. I mentioned that our friend could probably help him make his wig look more natural, but I dared not pry and possibly offend him. I did however, tell my wife that one day I planned to make the suggestion that Vertus shorten his hair and add a sprinkle of gray coloring. I had hoped that this would help him appear more natural. Perhaps Vertus would totally ignore me or even worse, suggest I pound sand on some deserted island. Though I constantly returned to the matter in my thoughts, I held my tongue for the time being.

YEARS LATER

I watched Vertus slow his pace. He no longer had the energy to work as hard. I began to assist him as much as I possibly could. He was wearing the wig one day and then the following day, out of the blue, something happened. Vertus appeared to have made a 180-degree turn. Without warning he was bald, his head shaved. Though he never admitted taking a razor and whacking off his hair, it sure looked that way. And the best part was that the wig was gone but not without a replacement. Vertus now wore a woolen knit cap that while growing up in my community became well known as a beanie.

When I looked at Vertus without the wig, I noticed the lower perimeter of his head; the portion visible beneath the beanie had no sign of hair growth. I assumed he shaved his head, because I never knew anyone to be naturally bald at the lower part of their scalp. In my mind I was elated. I thought to myself, Vertus has seen the light. He finally got it! I considered this a huge improvement and felt he was making real progress. Perhaps he received my telepathic message.

Vertus pictured while wearing a wig.

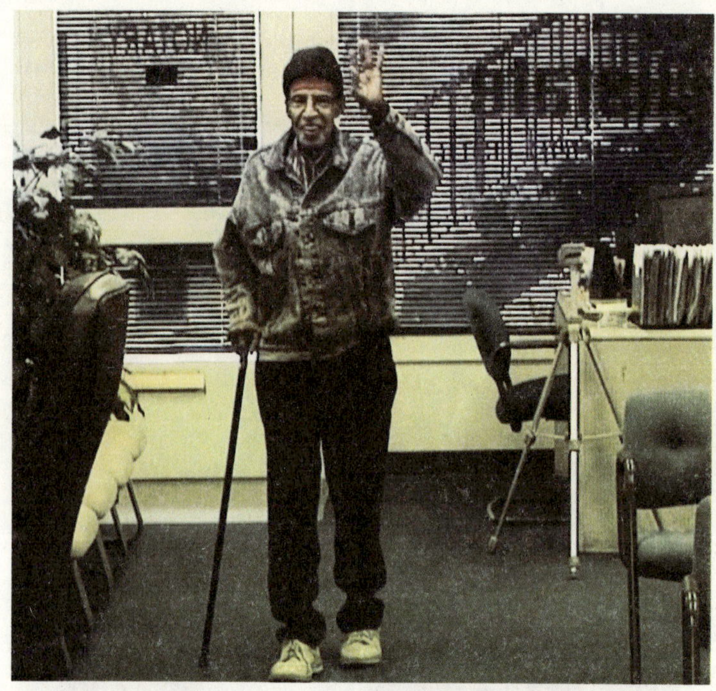

Vertus arrived in the office with a cheerful spirit.

This photo was taken during the time when I assumed Vertus shed his wig in favor of a new bald look. (Photo in 2006)

ALL THE TIME

After a while, it seemed strange that in place of the wig Vertus always wore his beanie. Just as I had never seen him without the wig before, I now never saw him without a beanie. He wore it to church while dressed in suit and tie—even when outside temperatures soared above 100 degrees. Whether at the bank, market or church, the look was the same.

Vertus wore a beanie in an array of colors, positioned to cover the top portion of his head, quite similar to the way one would wear a crown. Many times I tried to block it out, looking beyond the beanie. It was never easy, but I didn't want to pry. I could hear his response already, "I like wearing beanies. What's wrong with that?" Or reversing the question, "Why do you wear a tie or black shoes instead of brown?"

At the same time Vertus and I had bonded; we were as close as extended family. I invited him to attend my children's awards ceremonies, graduations and special holiday dinners. He always brought with him a sense of humor. Once I reenacted a speech about myself for Vertus word for word, "I go out of my way to avoid stepping on butterflies and could never burst a child's bubble with words denying the existence of Santa Claus." I went on, "I have no use for four letter words and enjoy giving to the less fortunate." I concluded, "I'm a straightforward compassionate guy who helps others help themselves." I thought I shared a mouth full, but Vertus, with a straight face, responded, "What does that mean?" He must have seen my face drop when he quickly added, "I was just kidding."

I told Vertus about my family outings like the trips to the drive-in movies, Disneyland and Knott's Berry Farm. I mentioned that while growing up I believed life was good. I told him how I believed my family would remain together forever. He was surprised to learn that I was once baptized Catholic and faithfully followed the religious doctrine. He was amazed to learn that I came from a large family and had ten siblings.

We had in common a childhood love for building and exchanged stories of our earliest construction projects. We both had stories about the pain we each felt after smashing a finger, usually a thumb hit by a hammer. We shared the frustration with trying to keep pets, such as pigeons and rabbits, dry inside their cages following a downpour of rain during the winter months. We described feeble attempts to reinforce the roof with anything imaginable, desperate to keep the wet at bay.

Vertus laughed while sharing a story about his stopping at nothing to care for his rabbits. He said, "Wilbert, I tried sneaking them into the house once. It was cold outside and I could imagine them freezing. But mother got a smell of them and threatened to put me and the rabbits out if I ever brought them inside again." We both laughed, reminiscing on the innocence of childhood.

During this conversation we talked about music and sports as well. I told him I had a love for music, the French Horn in particular. I played the instrument beginning in the seventh grade school year and also sung in the church and school chorus. I shared the memory of bringing my instrument home and playing it for my siblings for the first time. Vertus responded, "I always wanted to play an instrument or do something grand like that. But times were hard during my youth and I was never afforded the opportunity. So as a youngster I wanted a job and dreamt of operating a shine business like the man at the train depot."

We couldn't leave out stories about sports. I told him I was an athlete thanks in part to the basketball hoop hanging from our garage, but it was music that played a higher role in my life. Vertus said he was not athletic, but instead he considered himself the shy nerdy type. As for his choice in music, he loved the sound of old time gospel. He once tied the two subjects together, "Wilbert, I've got athletic ability about as much as Lil' Richard could sing without screaming. He couldn't do it and nor could I."

I later learned there was more about Vertus' childhood that he was keeping from me. He had so many friends and admirers, but no one knew the truth about him. As for me, I always thought his life was about his positive spirit and philosophy, with little to do with tragedy and sorrow. I thought he was wise as a result of the good questions he asked and the wisdom to get answers from folks wiser than he.

I was reminded of the 1944 Ink Spots song, *Into Each Life Some Rain Must Fall.* In my life the rain was an occasional sprinkle, and I compared it to the downpour I would soon learn fell upon Vertus from a very young age.

Maybe it was my concern for Vertus that contributed to why he chose me to share his incredible story with. Once I learned the truth about him, it changed my life forever. Perhaps when you read the upcoming chapters, instead of sadness, you might be inspired. Hopefully you will never forget this story, especially when trivial matters seem to cause a ballistic reaction. A memorable lesson of peace, patience and forgiveness is forthcoming.

LIKE A FATHER AND FRIEND

Our relationship flourished. I became Vertus' primary financial advisor, while he was meeting with, and taking on a familiar role with my entire family. On occasion, he attended my children's school functions and I always introduced Vertus to others as a member of our family. Though it didn't happen consciously, I found myself initiating him as my surrogate father.

I was comforted by Vertus as he sometimes reminded me of my biological father. Out of nowhere, while we sat in my office looking over paperwork, he asked, "Wilbert, I've never heard you talk about your dad. Why is that?" His question stunned me for a moment. I didn't think he noticed. It was because my father rarely crossed my mind. But he was correct… I didn't ever mention him. I responded to Vertus, "You know, I lost my father twice and I've since trained myself not to think about it." With compassion on his face, he said, "Wilbert, tell me why."

I first made a point about my mother who was my positive parental role model. I told Vertus that if it were not for her and the resilient moral character she instilled in me, things might have turned out quite differently. I shared the times when she cradled her children and expressed that we were going to be fine and how she assured our father's return. Even though she was never certain, she always kept us positive and looking forward to his return.

My mother led our survival. She obtained a job paying slightly above minimum wage to care for all nine of my siblings. I told Vertus that I owed her so much that I felt it my duty to make her proud, accomplishing good deeds and becoming someone she would be delighted with. I then told the short story of my father who walked away from our family in 1966. I told Vertus about the bitterness I felt, because, after all, I was just a kid pretending to be older and more mature. I reacted to my father's absence by searching for a male to stand in for my missing father. As the oldest boy, I was forced to quickly mature. Vertus looked and listened, seemingly saddened by my story.

My few school activities were shortened due the need to get home and help with chores, completing my own homework before helping my siblings with theirs. At times I wondered whether I was capable of shouldering such responsibility. Just after high school graduation I met a man through work, Tom Walker, whose wisdom and counsel helped me. He told me, "The fruits of life hang on trees, waiting for someone with enough sense to reach up and pick." I adopted those words for myself and shared similar thoughts with my siblings.

Eight years passed without my seeing or hearing from my father. Then, in 1974, when I was 24, I saw my father again. He spoke very few words and appeared very nervous. We exchanged no hugs and shared no smiles. I was certainly surprised! I wanted to tell how much he had hurt me and how I failed to let it cost me early successes. I wanted to tell how in spite of it all, I finished college and had a good career and this I accomplished while assuming his parental responsibilities.

I wanted him to realize how tough it was to hold things together and how troubled I was about not living the stress free existence of a normal teen. But there was no time—he walked away after a mere five minutes. I told Vertus I was bitter, and from that point forward, whenever questions arose about my father I responded as if he were dead.

This answer defined my path of least resistance, the easiest way to ensure a change of subject. I recall first responding this way while attending the "Father and Son Night" awards banquet held at my middle (junior high) school. That night kids were proudly clinging to their fathers, but for my brother and I, we only had each other. When asked by other kids, "Where is your father?" I responded, "My father is dead." This became my response for years. My brother and I vowed never to attend another award banquet. It was too painful.

In 1976, I saw my father again. He just showed unannounced at a family picnic. None of the family knew what to say and maybe if we did, it would be only one word, "Why?" Again he quickly left after greeting each one of us and exchanging only a few words. Then exactly one year went by before tragedy struck. We were told that my father received a telephone call from someone he apparently knew. Within minutes, my father headed out the door pledging to return shortly, a pledge he would not fulfill.

Authorities found him the next morning locked inside the trunk of his car. He had been beaten mercilessly. We were told there was little chance of his surviving the beating that shattered his skull. His initial condition was diagnosed as grave. Doctors later declared him fortunate to have momentarily survived. His pulse was very faint while his head swelled to twice its normal size. Life hinged on a respirator and whatever miracle doctors could perform. For ten days he lay in a coma.

We faced the decision to remove him from machines; the hardest decision I have even been a part of. It chilled me to the bone to think that during my earlier years I declared him dead. Now, as an adult, I desperately wanted him to recover. My father died at the age of forty-eight, of lacerations to the brain. His murder was never resolved.

When I finished my story, Vertus sat with a straight face looking into my eyes. He said, "Wilbert, that is a lot to endure. You must know that God made you a strong man for a reason." Vertus went on to explain the importance of love and forgiveness. He shared with me bible verses and attributes to God. Through Vertus, I was learning to forgive my father, a transformation I was glad to embrace. Old feelings and thoughts were releasing, setting me on a better road towards forgiveness. Vertus was teaching me that it was never my place to judge another human being. He told me, "It's not your place to judge me…but whatever you decide to do about your father and his memory, remember somebody bigger than you and I always knows best."

When Vertus used the description "Somebody bigger than you and I," I shuddered. That was the exact title of the song I sung at my father's funeral. Of all the words Vertus could have chosen to make his point, he chose those. I continued to realize the special connection I had with him.

Said With a Song

As years passed, our friendship grew closer. Vertus appeared to be in good health and we continued to sing together in the choir. Singing was more than Sunday's task. Music was my way of unwinding, even after a hard week at the office. My wife and I soon developed a taste for Karaoke.

We found a favorite that would allow us to avoid cooking one night a week while at the same time provide entertainment. The Sand and Surf Restaurant Lounge hosted a wide array of Karaoke, with some surprisingly talented guests. While my wife and I never grabbed the microphone, we enjoyed listening in.

The Karaoke crowd consisted mostly of nine-to-five folks stopping by to start their weekend. Over time, regulars shared in a community of music and cheer. These were not the cry-in-your-beer kind of folks one might find at a bar. I became friends with many while we circled together to enjoy favorite tunes. The Motown sound was always my favorite. The songs reminded me of high school and college, when "Record Hops," were King. I remember well when a dollar gained admission to the hop; we danced to music by the Four Tops, Marvin Gaye, The Temptations, Supremes, Whispers, and Delfonics.

The Karaoke Lounge circulated a catalog of song titles, while patrons were encouraged to take part. There was a sign hanging on the wall, large letters that urged everyone to show respect toward performers, a rule that was strictly followed. People were always courteous and respectful.

One particular evening, as I headed out to the lounge, I was feeling especially overwhelmed and found myself confiding with my Karaoke friends about Vertus. I shared about his wisdom, humor and philosophy on love and forgiveness. I vividly recall their reactions, thinking I exaggerated his character. After that, somehow my relationship and feelings about Vertus became connected to the warm atmosphere of the Karaoke Lounge, and subsequently, through the music that played. The Karaoke Lounge eventually became the place I came to sort things out. Through this venue, I found additional inspiration that helped me piece together Vertus' story and his impact on my life through familiar songs with special meaning.

Vertus on a hot summer day wore this wool beanie topped by a wide brimmed safari hat. Even worst, during the hot days of summer, Vertus wore an additional wide brim safari hat atop the woolen beanie, even when outside temperatures soared above 105 degrees. If given the same set of circumstances, I believe I would have suffered heatstroke. (Photo in 2006)

This wide-brimmed sun hat was worn atop the wool beanie to provide added shield from the midday sun.

"If I am greedy, I will lose. I'm not going to spend every day of my remaining life holding onto something I can't take with me when I die."

-Vertus

THE REVEAL

Though our relationship had grown into a close friendship, I still couldn't bring myself to mention the beanie or wig to Vertus. I decided to leave the issue and focus on the good times we had, especially the positive impact Vertus was having in my life. By then several more years had slipped by.

Vertus reached eighty-three years old. Though he had slowed down even more, he was still sharp as a nail within his mind. Our friendship had reached a remarkable level. We had been friends for over twenty years, and Vertus became more and more like father to me. I began to look after him more and more as he showed signs of aging, and loneliness. I tried to offset this by welcoming him more often to my home and office. Vertus was personally invited to attend every major holiday function.

He never told me he was lonely, but I heard it in his voice and saw the change in him. He was a workaholic, serving on multiple boards for various homeowner associations, in which he owned condos. He simultaneously held multiple posts at the church as well. I saw this as his attempt to confirm his worth and connect with people whom he could love like family.

One day, however, during one of our weekly visits, Vertus' behavior seemed strange. It was about 2 o'clock on a Friday afternoon. I was standing just inside my office doorway. He appeared exhausted from the day's heat and had sweat falling from his brow. Vertus walked right past my employees and hesitantly glanced their way, but he did not respond to their greetings. Instead, he walked directly toward me, as if he carried a heavy burden. As I watched this all unfold, I felt something was not right.

As Vertus entered my office, he oddly never looked up at me. He stared at the floor, purposely avoiding eye contact. I immediately offered him a chair directly in front of my desk. Just behind his chair was a picture window, about four-by-four foot in diameter. The window provided a view of my office. Staff could look in and see my face along with the backside view of Vertus, who, for some reason, continued to avoid looking at me.

My mind was uneasy. This was not like the hundreds of times before when he visited my office. Something was terribly wrong. My mind raced in paranoia. I wondered if Vertus was ill. Did someone injure him? Was there a death in his family or a tragic fire at one of his rentals? Did someone rob him after learning about his inclination to carry large sums of cash? I uttered, "Vertus, are you ok?" He looked at me and there were tears streaming down his face. This startled me! I thought he was about to share something dreadful at any moment.

He said, "I miss my family in Indiana. My parents and grandparents are gone, and I find little reason to visit." When I asked him about returning home, he said, "I couldn't let myself go back. There is so much there I just can't handle." He continued, "I have tormented myself for a long time while searching for the courage to tell you my secret. It involves why I always covered my head and hid it all my life. I've never told anyone my secret, and now, I think I want to tell you."

It hurt me so to see his tears. My stomach tightened in anticipation of whatever had befallen him. I needed Vertus to talk to me now! I got up from my desk and came to his side. He removed his horn-rimmed glasses, looked at me, then through a faint utterance said, "Wilbert, I'm just tired." Having no clue as to what he was referring to, I responded, "Tired of what?" He then started to cry with more emotion, losing control. My friend was in so much pain about something very serious. I never before saw him cry. I suspected the worst and did not rule out the possibility of dialing 911 for help.

I really thought he may have been robbed and sensed heavy uneasiness, as though whoever the perpetrators, they were in the room with us. Vertus responded, "When I was a boy, just five years old, I was experimented on." Continuing his vocal struggle, he added, "I was just a child, a little boy; I was not some sort of animal." Now I was even more confused. "Wow!" was all I could think. What would come next?

I sat by his side in the chair next to him. I was not sure of my reaction, still grappling to understand. I knew Vertus well, but I asked myself if he might be in the midst of a mental breakdown? I wondered where this story might end and what do I do when he adds an outlandish part like this happened aboard a spaceship where an unwelcomed invasion entered his mind or body. I stalled for moments while I regained my composure and then went over to close my office door.

For the first time since walking into my office that day, Vertus looked at me while he dried his tears. I assumed he awaited my reaction before deciding to tell me more. "Vertus what did they do to you?" I prompted, knowing that if I cracked the slightest smile or gave any hint that I did not believe him, he might think I was mocking him. This would only lead him to retreat to the very place he just mustered the courage to come out from. I suggested he take his time and tell me more. This seemed for the moment to calm him. I asked, "You said you were experimented on as a little boy." He replied. "Yes, they experimented on us with radiation."

Before now I thought that Vertus was in perfect health. I believed his laughter and pleasant thoughts and thought I knew everything about him. Then before I could think of what next to say, Vertus uttered the invitation, "Do you want to see what I'm talking about?" Without hesitation I responded, "Yes!" I knew that whatever Vertus was about to show me, lied just beneath his beanie. In fact, I would soon learn that what I was about to see, no more than five persons outside his medical doctors had ever seen.

Vertus first removed the wide brimmed hat followed by his beanie. I sat motionless while my suggestions that he stop wearing the wig for cosmetic improvement flashed across my mind. I was concerned about simple cosmetics when for decades greater, deeper rationales were at play, hiding who he really was. All this began to race through my mind, surfacing like vapors from a boiling kettle. My heart sank in shame. I felt embarrassed for thinking so superficially.

Vertus shown removing his beanie.

When he took his beanie off, I couldn't believe my eyes. His head was heavily speckled by the loss of skin pigmentation and oddly shaped. Vertus' head resembled the symmetry of a cucumberem dash no spaces tall on the top and slender on the side. There was no hair except a few strands near his left ear. I saw scarring across the entire width of his forehead, just above the eyebrows. The right front quadrant of his scalp was whitest due to a loss of skin color. Both his ears were wafer thin and bore blemishing across their upper edges.

Atop his wound laid a medical cover sponge measuring 4-by-2 inches in diameter. The cover sponge was fused onto whatever it was there to protect. Vertus began to meticulously tug along the periphery of the sponge in an attempt to detach it. Once removed, it exposed a horrific wound that resembled raw tattered flesh containing numerous peaks and valleys. Its color was a vibrant pink flesh tone, shadowed by yellow pus-looking pockets. Discharges secreted from various points of his scalp coupled with a mildly stale odor. If I had not seen this for myself, I'm not certain I could have identified this as a human scalp.

As the cover sponge dislodged, it tore away scabs that caused bleeding. Blood streamed from various points down into his face. When I saw his bleeding, I opened my office door and headed for the washroom. I moved calmly, very careful not to cause any attention. I wanted to avoid anyone from peeking in and hoped no one was paying attention to my office window. Once in the washroom, I pulled paper towels, wet a few and within seconds returned to him. I handed him the wet towels and felt helpless in my ability to render additional aid.

To my surprise, Vertus calmly blotted both his scalp and face convincing me that this was no emergency. Most likely this was a routine occurrence. But for me, I was nervous and filled with anxiety. I again closed the office door and was not certain what to say.

For the first time in over twenty years, I felt distance between us; not unfamiliarity about what I knew about him, but about what I didn't know about him. I felt misfortune for Vertus and whatever this thing was growing on his scalp. It seemed to live and thrive while overwhelming him. It's hard to believe that after twenty years of standing so close to Vertus, that I was seeing his head uncovered for the first time. I again asked, "Who did this to you?" He did not answer. In my heart I knew the answer would eventually come and I needed to be patient. He said, "I have suffered a lot of pain and I am tired of carrying this burden!"

We were silent for about a minute. I tried to make it obvious that this moment belonged to him, and him alone. This time it was I who avoided eye contact. He said, "The hospital needed to know human reactions to radiation exposure. They experimented on ten children; I was one of them. It happened in a small town in Indiana during 1927. We all attended a small school located in a township named Lyles Station. It was my first day of school."

"They told us we were going on a field trip. We ended up in a hospital basement. The radiation was applied to my head, causing the wound I suffer today and for the past eighty years; the radiation has caused my scalp to deteriorate. The treatments (experiments) were given under false pretenses, orchestrated by the very community leaders (school superintendent and head medical doctor at the county hospital) the poor families trusted. We were promised a new cure for scalpel ringworm, a promise used to hide their true motive." Vertus continued, "My parents didn't have a clue what was about to happen. Those people viewed me and the other children as dollar signs."

Frankly, I was not certain I believed everything I was hearing. But on the other hand I knew something terrible caused his condition. Vertus went on, "It happened in the hospital's basement. There was a contamination of ringworm at the school. They put us on a school bus and took us to the hospital to cure the ringworm—so we all thought!" He went on to tell the haunting phrase he has heard reverberating within his psyche since age five. A phrase he says wakes him up at night, words spoken by a technician that left in her wake a little boy forced to suffer this wound for a lifetime. "Oh my God! I've given him too much."

I sat quiet staring at the wall. I needed a moment to process all of the information I had just heard. I told Vertus I was deeply sorry for the misfortune that was inflicted upon him. He immediately interjected, "Wilbert, I don't want pity. That's the one thing I've feared my whole life." Then I asked him, "What can I do to help?" I committed myself to helping him and assured him that whatever he needed, I would be there to help. With sincerity, he looked me straight in the eyes and said, "Help me Wilbert. I am getting old and tired. This burden is getting too much for me now." He began to cry again. Silently tears rolled down his face. I gave him a hug. He no longer had to carry this burden alone.

When he left, I was there alone with my thoughts, and I was not very kind to myself. You could only imagine what I felt. It was none of my business why he wore a wig, hat or beanie. And then I realized how much I really didn't want to know why he did.

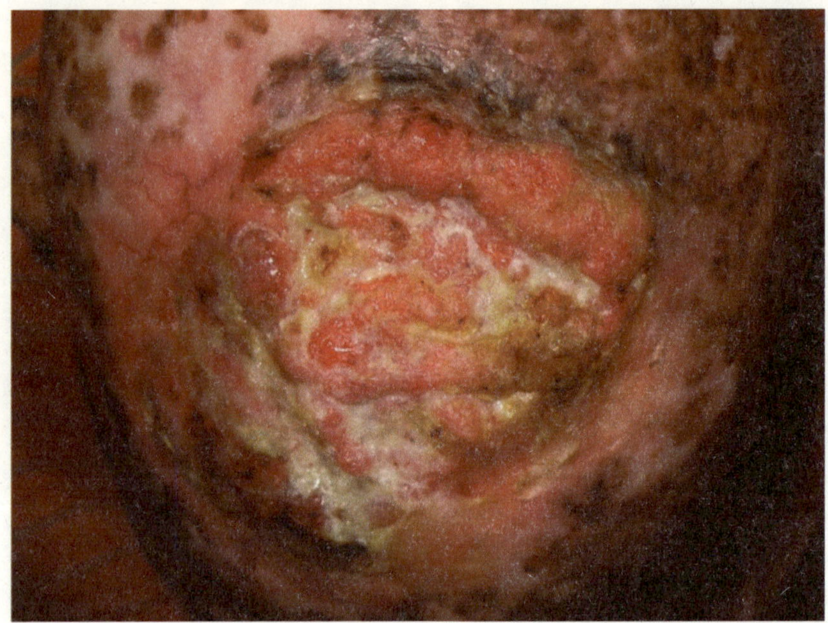

Standing in front of Vertus, this shot of his scalp was taken just following my first interview with him. It shows his scalp as Vertus tilts his head forward while looking down upon his lap. (Photo 2006)

The cover sponge that simply laid atop Vertus' wound. (Photo 2006)

Peeling Back Layers

The story Vertus laid out to me was heart wrenching, and the fact that he was so young made it more horrific. It was hard to believe this was about curing ringworm, such a minor fungus. And the idea that the technician knew she had given Vertus too much radiation also added to my distress. Vertus told me, "I've relived that moment so many times. I could not stop the nightmares where I envisioned her using my head as an ironing board. In those dreams the technician rested an iron on my head and left me to suffer."

Hearing Vertus describe this was difficult, and even worse as I wondered how he has hid this all his life. What an indescribable loneliness Vertus must have endured until now, having had nobody in which to confide. What dug deepest was the fact that I drew such attention to the small, trivial things like the color of his hair and the shape of his wig. I only made it more difficult for him to go along unnoticed. Now I was recruited, and a part of this secret which rested hidden beneath such an insignificant issue of vanity.

I realized how much Vertus must care for me to keep me in his life for so many years and ultimately confide in me. To this day, I continue to wonder why he chose me. Everything now made perfect sense. The style of his wig was not the discretion of a barber with unlimited options. Instead it was the hand Vertus was dealt by the radiation. Vertus shared his own insecurity when he described it, "My head is shaped like a doll's head. It resembles the shape of a cucumber!"

I was nauseated thinking about what it must be like to hide from those not willing to see him as he really was? I was becoming more frustrated as I thought about it. All we have to do is be comfortable with him and let him be. Such a simple compromise would bring such happiness. All of us who have met him and known him, owed Vertus a huge debt, and I was already contemplating how I was going to repay him. I could not ignore the question of how he kept this from me for decades. I was astonished that during our twenty years of closeness, I never once heard him complain. I knew better than to criticize him, and that day I vowed never to again judge another.

That evening while at home, I was not my usual talkative self. But, eventually, I found the courage to share my experience with my wife. The pain was so real that I cried while describing the events. I selectively recounted parts of his story, already being protective of Vertus. I was duty-bound not to violate his trust, even with my wife. I knew that my reaction had as much to do with my guilt. My wife suggested that I try to learn from this life lesson and move on. I'm certain this would have been my advice to her if the shoe were on the other foot. This time, though, it wasn't enough. No one could have seen the beginnings of what boiled up inside of me; I needed answers for Vertus—what exactly happened, and why?

When dinner was served, I poked a fork around my plate but ate very little. In bed, I got little sleep. When I dozed, it was while struggling through a maze of anger. The following night, my wife tried to cheer me up. She took me to our Karaoke Lounge, hoping we could have fun as we had on many previous occasions. This didn't help at all. Every song somehow referenced Vertus. I continued to ask myself how any man could be so cruel to a young child. I couldn't enjoy myself there either. I just wanted to get back to talking with Vertus.

I asked Vertus if I could stop by the following morning. I'd picked up some breakfast for us, although my portion sat unattended. Without prompting him, Vertus continued on the topic. "A bit of my dignity and self-esteem is lost every time I look at myself through the mirror," he said. I hated this. I thought about how Vertus never once said he was owed anything, but at a minimum, I concluded, somebody owed him a huge apology for eighty years of agony. The only way to accomplish this was to get back to where his story began. Vertus was again forcing me to grow in greater awareness.

During my life, I was the one that summarized and extracted life lessons from the situations of others and helped friends and family make sense of it. But when it came to Vertus, it seemed like I was always the one being helped. He continually ministered *The Golden Rule*: Do unto others, as you would wish them to do unto you. We all share certain inherent rights because we are members of the human race. Human beings are individually different, coming in different genders, sizes, shapes and colors. I couldn't believe that this simple rule was the one most obviously violated when it came to the children of Lyles Station.

Vertus was paying too much for his right to survive. The only way that I could conceptualize all that he had been through was to focus on the lesson one could learn from his experience. I became intrigued by his story and I wanted to learn more. Knowledge became my consolation. I figured the only way I could possibly make it better was to give a voice to Vertus' story so that it could never happen again. I asked if we could talk about the ordeal further. I realized it was a touchy issue for him and didn't want to cause him any extra strain. Although reluctant and understandably nervous, Vertus agreed to return to my office the following day around 6 pm.

Vertus told me that he wanted me to realize that discussing his childhood was in contrast to long-held practices to bury the experiments. "I have never shared this with anyone," he said, "Only four people outside my doctors have ever seen my head. Even my immediate family has not seen the deterioration that has occurred."

I could not help comparing this story with the syphilis study at

Tuskegee, a time most Americans choose to forget. The study involved an experiment carried out prior to World War II, when the U.S. denied needed medication to known carriers of syphilis. Those affected were given medical examinations but were never told they were infected with syphilis.

I told Vertus I wanted to learn more about the other nine children that were with him during the experiments. I craved their accounts and wanted to know if they were alive and well? I was not certain I could even find them, but in addition to locating them, I wanted to see the hospital that did this and locate the school Vertus attended. I hoped to find anyone capable of answering the questions that would help connect the dots of this story.

About a week later I telephoned Vertus. We exchanged the usual pleasantries, and got caught up on all the latest events. Cutting me short, he said, "Wilbert, I bet you think I'm as crazy as a Betsy-Bug, don't you?" I responded, "No Vertus; not at all. I actually think you're remarkably brave and resilient." He needed to hear that I believed in him and cared just as much. And I wanted him to feel comfortable and open to share even more with me. My goal was to keep him contributing information so that I could somehow understand how this event was allowed to happen.

Getting more pieces of the puzzle began with a visit the following day. At first Vertus was uneasy and apprehensive. He said to me, "Wilbert, I'm not certain that I have the strength. I've always tried to forget about this." I assured him that I understood his feeling and shared with him my need for someone to make sense of it all. I wanted to share his story with the world. I said, "Vertus how about meeting me tomorrow?" He replied, "I will let you know." Within that response I heard his struggle. On one hand he feared uncovering the painful memories while also wanting answers to long-held questions best uncovered by our collaboration. After much questioning, he agreed to meet.

The next day Vertus was surprisingly poised, in no real hurry to talk. He came to my office as he always did. It was a mild summer day and the sun had cast a shadow in the evening sky. He sat with his fingers interlaced and both hands resting on his lap. Vertus made jokes about the real estate market. I shared some tips I had read about investing. Then I said to him, "Vertus I've known you for a long time and feel you are a part of my family. You know my wife and have watched my children grow into adulthood." I had something I needed to confess.

I admitted to him that my thoughts about his wig and beanie were not always kind. I said, "I ridiculed you within my subconscious mind." I continued, "Then after hearing your truthfulness, it ripped my heart out. You have again taught me a valuable lesson. I want you to allow me to tell this story of you and how you have impacted my life. It would be my honor to share your life, and the lessons you've taught me, with others."

I told Vertus I was certain he had a special ministry to share with the world. The shoe was now on the other foot—I was the one crying the tears of sorrow. Maybe I was doing the meager job of managing the moment. I flashed back to the time I briefly ran into my father after his many years of absence, how I wanted to feel his embrace but could not force it. I pulled Vertus to me and proceeded to place my arm around his shoulders. At that point, I walked him to the door and just before he exited, he said, "Let me think about it. I'll let you know."

When Vertus walked out the door, he took with him my sorrow. I was certain he feared making the wrong decision. Perhaps this was a breaking point for him, similar to what first led him to my door to share his story. I knew I was good for him, helping him to shoulder the experiment and aftereffects, something he was no longer willing or able to carry alone. At the same time I wanted him to know just how good he'd been to me, and I wanted to repay him for the terrible part I played.

THE ANTICIPATION

During the days that followed, it was difficult for me to focus on much beyond the experiments. I anxiously waited for Vertus' permission to write his story, slightly intimidated by the potential task ahead. I had no practical experience as a writer beyond the occasional research project or op-ed piece published in my local newspaper, but if given the green light, I was willing to give it my very best. I knew it was important to be patient and not apply any unreasonable pressure on Vertus while awaiting his decision.

Days seemed like weeks. One night while anticipating his response, I dreamed about a young boy sitting beneath a radiation device that was placed upon his head. The boy was strapped to a chair and screamed out in pain. I fought through the crowd of onlookers trying to reach him. The boy was crying; his head burned by the radiation. The boy reached out unsuccessfully for anyone able to rescue him. I fought valiantly and eventually stopped the flow of radiation. I then employed a comforting embrace, holding the boy securely. I awakened from that dream sweating, ignited by an even stronger passion to work with Vertus. This particular dream was frequent.

It was now about five days since I last spoke with Vertus. I knew I would see him at church on Sunday but decided that calling him would be the day's highest priority. When I entered my office I dialed his number. "Hello Vertus how are you today? I called to check on you." As though not hearing my words, Vertus responded with his own line of questioning. "If you wrote some sort of book, how would you learn about the story? Where would we meet and how often?" I responded, "How frequently would you like to meet?" Vertus replied, "I guess we can work that out later. For now, I'm going to trust you. Let's do it." I was feeling both elated and terrified.

Now what do I do, I thought as I hung up the phone.

I began to study the particulars on writing a biography. I found suggested questions designed to 'break the ice' and prepare a story to be professional, honest and organized. Though it seemed I had known Vertus forever, I wasn't completely relaxed and felt an unspoken status of probation. He might change his mind if things did not progress to his liking or refuse to continue with the project at a moment's notice. I felt it best to speak freely in the beginning, ditching any formal questions that would create a formal tone. I wanted Vertus to feel open to speak with me. I gathered my camcorder, tripod and a handful of tapes and sat down to record the first of many interviews.

I encouraged him to talk as much as possible. I began asking about those pleasurable times of his childhood. I wanted to avoid things like the experiments, deferring that until later. He told me about school and the many games they played as children and how after what was done to him, he still found a way to live a memorable childhood. I asked about pastimes like baseball, or pleasantries associated with the larger school experience. But no matter how much I tried to avoid it, we found ourselves drawn to the experiments, a testament to the enormous impact it had on his life.

The sharpness of his memory became apparent; Vertus remembered incredible amounts of detail. It was as if he read a list of facts etched onto the back of his hand. At first, we recorded for about one hour and made small talk. We laughed and joked about his favorite memories of home and his family. Vertus shared stories about going to church as a family and their love and reverence for God. He spoke of impressive meals his mother prepared, even when their food supply was low. He even shared a funny story about the time he cried during his church's Easter play when they dramatically crucified Jesus. As a young boy, he thought they were killing Jesus right in front of him, which made him very sad.

He recalled his family's response. "My brother teased me about that incident for years." Lastly, he joked about how his parents taught him lessons in savings. He said his father would give him a nickel for his help on the family farm. His father instructed him to hide it in a safe place so he could find it when he needed it. So he buried it in the backyard thinking it would be safe and had the hardest time digging it up when it came time to spend it. Through his laughter he added, "I worked harder digging to find the money than I did while earning it."

I recall the glow that appeared as Vertus saw himself for the first time on camera, reviewing the video playback. It was obvious that his demeanor changed whenever the discussion centered on a man's inability to show love and compassion for others. This always made him sad, troubling him deeply. He said, "I don't understand why as children they did not see us as special, somehow not deserving what we got." But, he took the hand he was dealt and proved his worth through good deeds and many accomplishments.

It was unbelievable that Vertus worked the same job forty years without ever missing a single day of work, while also working a second job for twenty of those years with perfect attendance. I was overwhelmed to learn that as he walked the corridors of county hospital all those years, he entered rooms where x-ray and radiation were commonplace. Following the boyhood experiment, this took unimaginable courage.

Our weekly talks spanned months. Some days were better than others, and yes, there was the occasional headache or related ailment that got in the way. At times, the burning in his head would reach intolerable levels, Vertus describing the feeling as tantamount to the burn on a hand from a hot stove. I was never impatient with him and always allowed his thoughts to surface at a comfortable pace. One day while filming, the discussion got to be too heavy. Vertus stopped mid sentence and said, "Let's keep this taping short, Wilbert. I want to go home to rest and perhaps you should take a break yourself." I respected Vertus' request and didn't press anything further. I packed up the equipment and dropped him off at home.

Vertus was amused at his character when he viewed himself on camera for the first time. (Photo 2006)

I decided to visit the Karaoke Lounge. I wanted to unwind, relax and be entertained with topics other than Vertus. But again, I couldn't separate my mind from Vertus' story. So many unanswered questions and missing pieces ran through me. I drowned out most of the conversations at the table and tried putting the pieces together in my head. Then a song played that drew my attention to its lyrics. The song was an original, written by a patron.

I want to go back, back to put it all together
I want to see, if it's just a cloud in my mind
Gotta go back, back to the place it all began
Come go with me, Just you and me

I clapped to cheer him on. During the excitement, I had an epiphany. It hit me like a ton of bricks. In order to do this project justice and really tell the story in its entirety, I would need more: more information, more research, more details and more footage. In order for this story to be correct, Vertus and I needed to return to Lyles Station, the place where it all began.

I stayed up most of the night and couldn't wait to ask Vertus if he would be willing to go back to Lyles Station, Indiana. The next morning I called him at the crack of dawn. He picked up the phone and after our usual greetings, he asked, "So, what's got you up and running so early this morning?" Getting right to the point, I replied. "Vertus, how would you feel about traveling back to Lyles Station? I know you have not returned back for a visit in many years. It would be good. We could arrange to visit your remaining family members. I would love to meet them all and get their input on this story."

Vertus was quiet for a minute, as if taking it all in. I prepared to continue talking, hoping to persuade him, but he started talking first. He said, "Wilbert, you're right. I have not gone back in years." I continued, "Vertus, we don't have to go now. We could arrange to travel sometime within the next month or so. Think about it and let me know." Just as calm as he answered the phone he replied back immediately, "Wilbert, I don't see it as a bad idea. If it will help the project, then I'll go. Plus it would be good to see my family."

His acceptance had me elated. I got off the phone and immediately began putting an itinerary together for our trip. I prepared by first speaking with Vertus' brother Melvin and first cousin Horace Hardiman over the phone. I told them that Vertus and I would be coming to visit soon and would like to meet with them. I informed them of my current research and asked if I could interview them to learn more about the experiments of 1927. I was excited to expand the characters in this story and the men seemed impressed to know that I was coming cross-country just to meet them. They were also amazed to think I would meet them to discuss a subject they believed died decades before. They both shared that they didn't think that the unfortunate events of the experiment would interest anyone anymore.

I hoped that the quick wit and incredible recall Vertus had, the other men would share. I also hoped that the men would be comfortable in reliving their experiences without shutting down. I was excited and couldn't wait to meet his brother Melvin, uncle Gletus, cousins Horace and Melvin "Fuzz" Hardiman. I intended to record every detail and ask questions that would allow the men to see just how much I cared about their story. I arranged chats with local agencies, booked study sessions in the town library and had the librarian set books aside that might further my research. I also planned to search out the city and county archives.

Above Wilbert interviews Vertus in his office. (Photo 2006)

Burrowing Through History

Once the travel arrangements were made, I began to research all I could in preparation for my visit to Lyles Station. I was eager to better understand who the "they" were that made up this historic community. Internet and phone research became my daily focus. I wanted to be sure I had all the information I would need to make my trip a success. To start, I was able to confirm the identity of all ten students experimented on in 1927. There were nine Hardimans and one Stewart, nine boys and one girl. Five victims were alive and five deceased. All ten are listed below. Those alive when I began the story are marked with an asterisk.

Allan F. Hardiman

Garwood V. Hardiman

Gletus R. Hardiman*

Ella Mae Hardiman

Horace M. Hardiman*

Lloyd Hardiman

Melvin C. Hardiman*

Melvin L. Hardiman*

Vertus W. Hardiman*

Milburn Stewart

Next, I traced the Hardiman family history. I searched through online databases, archived records and previously conducted conversations with Vertus. During these hours, I learned that the Hardiman family had a rich history of achievement beginning with Vertus' great grandfather James Hardiman, born in 1825. James along with brothers Alexander and Fuller came to Lyles from Tennessee. Their father was a white Virginia farmer and their mother was a housemistress. As the Civil War approached, the three brothers were transported across the Ohio River to a free territory to avoid slavery. Slavery was the critical issue of the day, and the sacrifice made by their father ensured that the Hardiman boys would never be slaves, a critical point in the Hardiman history.

Their father moved his boys to Lyles Station, the small Negro settlement affectionately referred to as "Freedom Village." This was also a main artery in route to Canada where freedom awaited runaway slaves. The township was recognized as a colony founded and settled by freed men and escaped slaves. The settlement at its peak during years 1880-1913 grew to about a thousand residents. Mr. Joshua Lyles, the town's founder, needed a local post office and train stop (depot) to significantly enhance population growth, so in 1870, he received both the post office and train stop in exchange for six acres of land. In 1886 the settlement was officially named Lyles Station in honor of Mr. Lyles.

James Hardiman became a successful farmer, ultimately owning hundreds of acres of local farmland. He strongly advocated education as the key to a better life and wanted the best for his family. He believed strongly in hard work and self-sufficiency. I found records of him farming crops of corn and melons. In 1898, Vertus' father Claude Hardiman was also born in Lyles Station. Along with wife Irene, Claude built their family home. They were hard workers, which is, apparently, where Vertus learned the principle of hard work.

This early photo of the Hardimans was taken at the turn of the century. (Photo circa 1900)

Vertus was born in 1922. Claude and Irene traveled four miles east to nearby Gibson General hospital located in Princeton, Indiana, to give birth to twin boys, Vertus Welborn and Curtis James Hardiman. Vertus was the second of four children born to his parents, he had an older brother Melvin and a younger brother Curtis (his identical twin), and a sister, Vera. The family experienced tragedy when their infant son Curtis, Vertus' twin-brother, died at 8 months of age as a result of a severe case of whooping cough.

Their home environment was similar to most during those times. They lived in a rather plain three bedroom, two-story house with enough space for basic family comfort. There was farmland surrounding the house, but not enough to allow a comfortable income for the family. To supplement farming, Vertus' father Claude took a second job at the local railway depot where he worked as a janitor. Vertus remembered, "Around the farm we always had chores, as early as I could remember."

His mother was a typical 1920's farmer's wife. From the kitchen to the storage shed, washing, ironing, cooking, cleaning, churning butter and mending clothes, her work was never done. Vertus told stories of how Irene prepared meals on an old wood-burning stove; a process that began each dawn when she hauled firewood for cooking. He told me about the smokehouse, saying, "It was a place that was a meat smoker and a storage house because refrigeration had not been invented."

Vertus was truly touched by the memory of his mother. He said, "She religiously prepared three meals every day. She cooked the meals all at once eliminating the need to ignite the early style cooking stove multiple times a day." He told how this practice was appreciated most in the hot summer months, avoiding the enormous build up of heat in the house.

In that part of the country the early meal was known as breakfast, the midday meal called dinner and the final meal was referred to as supper. Following supper, the family usually went to bed early to get a head start on the next day's early rise. Vertus had fond memories of activities just before bedtime. Irene usually read a book or played a game with them.

Eventually the family was able to save enough to purchase a radio that quickly became a major source of entertainment and awareness. Vertus identified life as good. Within the Lyles community, fellow residents respected each other and made it a point to lift up their brother, in contradiction to the treatment received from some outsiders. They found strength by leaning on each other during the challenges of the early twentieth century.

Faith and their belief in God were inseparable doctrines. On Sunday morning, the township found fellowship at nearby Wayman Chapel. In churches outside Lyles Station, color lines were sharply drawn. Negroes were seldom allowed to fully participate, usually relegated to seating in a designated loft.

Irene holds Vertus along with husband Claude who holds their other son Melvin. (Photo circa 1923)

There was plenty of family; Irene and Claude had their brothers and sisters in addition to other relatives that represented multiple generations living in Lyles Station. Each generation gave birth to a host of offspring. There were big family dinners on Sunday afternoon that included games such as log rolling, horseshoe pitching and corn husking. Vertus spoke fondly stating, “I couldn’t wait to become bigger and stronger so I could participate.”

I asked Vertus about his childhood and he replied, “I did not have much of a childhood, because in those days there was a lot to do on the farm.” He told me that school was the place children played and generally not at home. Of course, when you consider that, school was very popular. Vertus added, "My father was a serious man who taught that in order to have anything worthwhile, it would require you working extra hard to achieve it." I asked Vertus more about Claude and his principles. He responded with the following story about a boyhood incident that landed him in trouble.

He told about a bigger boy that lived down the road. One afternoon the young boy cursed at Vertus in the worst kind of way and given the times, one of the words used was the "n" word. In retaliation Vertus hurled a rock that struck the boy who reacted with noticeable anger and charged after Vertus. In an attempt to escape the boy's fury, Vertus ran like the wind, but was shortly caught. Vertus fought with the boy but suffered a pretty good "walloping". Following the scuffle, even with scrapes and bruises, Vertus felt proud of himself. He said while laughing out loud, "I didn't think the boy would ever use that word again."

But when he got home his mother asked what happened. Vertus was honest and described the event. When Claude arrived, Vertus again recounted the story. Claude reacted strongly, "Your mistake was greater than that of the other boy, because you threw the rock." Claude concluded, the boy was 49% wrong and you were 51% wrong. Vertus said, "It was a profound lesson, that words cannot cause a bloody nose." Vertus shared this story with pride.

Vertus completed thoughts of his childhood by recounting a baseball story wherein he was assigned the role of pitcher. "My aim was so bad, I couldn't hit a bull in the butt with a bass fiddle. Ante-Over was my favorite game. We threw a ball over a house, while shouting… A-n-t-e-O-v-e-r. If the other team caught it, they raced around the house and tried to hit (capture) a member of the other team with the ball."

It didn't take long for me to start burning more than my fair share of midnight oil. I found myself substituting research for sleep. But I was eager to learn more about the family and discover the virtue that held them together through the hardships they faced.

An early photo of Hardimans following the Sunday morning worship. (Photo circa 1921)

Vertus' boyhood home features a pond about fifty yards from the main house where today cattle graze and wade.

With a growing settlement came the need for worship and Wayman Chapel A.M.E. Church was formed. It is recorded that of all the churches, the African Methodist Episcopal Church has perhaps done more to enhance the freedom and emancipation of Negros than any other. Wayman Chapel AME Church in Lyles Station was founded in 1887 and then remodeled in 1957. It provided a foundation for many early settlers.

EDUCATION, A KEY INGREDIENT

As my research intensified, one topic kept surfacing in the Hardiman family history. It centered on the importance of education and its role in developing their character and drive for achievement. It began with the school in Lyles Station where the ringworm contamination took place. Values held by this school were central to the community's overall values on education.

As a young boy, Vertus and other children, did exactly what approving adults would have hoped for them; they remained focused on good schooling. This basic premise was an important factor for understanding the underlying value of education in Lyles. People who settled there, fought hard for it, ultimately establishing the Lyles Station Consolidated School, built in 1922. Vertus continually shared how that school played an essential role in shaping his character.

The first school at Lyles Station was established about 1865. It was housed in a log cabin and the instructional cost for each student was one dollar per month to attend. All students assembled in a single room with large windows to allow as much natural lighting as possible. There were no lamps, nor artificial lighting to aid study.

Hardiman parents and adults learned side by side with their kids. They were as committed to learning as their children. Arm-twisting was never called for to encourage attendance. Parents saw their own need for learning, just as they did for their children. At that time, it was believed that the Negro race was educationally deficient; subsequently, community leaders saw an importance in emphasizing education for all.

The newly constructed consolidated school was initially multi-racial. The small township at its peak represented only fifty-five homes, leaving extra seats at the new school. Non-Negro students living outside the boundaries of Lyles Station filled those seats. Vertus shared a story about the key reason the school became segregated.

In 1923 a white student received punishment administered by a black teacher. White parents felt the punishment was too severe and subsequently, school officials felt it best to transfer all white students out of Lyles Station into nearby schools. The move left only Negros as schoolchildren at the new facility. The school was home to approximately 50 students, many from the Hardiman family.

This is one of the earliest known photos of Ms. Nannie Bell, Lyles Station schoolmarm. (Photo circa 1870)

This is the oldest known photo of Mrs. Nannie Bell's class at the Lyles Station School. Here Mrs. Bell is pictured approximately 50 years after the earlier photo where she now poses alongside her class in 1920. Pictured on the bench, second from the right is Edna Frye, the 96 year-old who later contributes to this story.

Above is the original consolidated school building constructed in 1922. It remained abandoned for forty years before its 1997 restoration. The school now serves as a living history museum.

The Lyles Station Historic Preservation Corporation led the effort in 2002 to restore the school.

Vertus had wonderful memories of the school's first teacher and principal, Mr. Joseph Lucas. He was simply known as Uncle Joe, a true uncle to he and most of the students, either by blood or marriage. Uncle Joe was married to Vertus' aunt, Florence. Vertus said, "Uncle Joe knew of the limited opportunities his Negro students had, but he still challenged us to advance beyond harsh realities. In return we trusted Uncle Joe and academically outperformed even the white students across the state."

The school received no state or federal funding, relying on fish fries, cookouts and bake sales for funding. Though resources were scarce, Uncle Joe found ways to get the job done. Secondhand school supplies were handed down by more favored schools. Lyles subsequently never saw new desks, books, team uniforms or other equipment. Parents invested trust and faithful support to Uncle Joe, contributing a little extra money whenever they could. In exchange, he instilled in each Lyles Station student the belief that they were somebody special.

Joseph A. Lucas

Joseph A. Lucas (Uncle Joe), the only Principal Lyles Station Consolidated School had during its existence, 1922-1958.

Vertus' memory was vivid. I laughed when he described the school outhouse, located at the rear of the property about fifty feet from the main building. When Vertus described how, during that era corncobs functioned as toilet paper, I could only shake my head in disbelief. Each outhouse contained an ample supply of corncobs, both red and white in color. The red cob was used first, and did most of the work, followed by the white cob, which provided a visual confirmation of one's success.

Vertus shared fond memories of a huge front yard and long walkway leading from the main road to the school's front door. Uncle Joe found an ideal use for the walkway. It became the divide to separate boys from girls. The boys played on the east lawn and the girls on the west. Uncle Joe's office was located on the second floor of the school, a perfect vantage point to spot potential rule violators.

On the last day of the school year, traditions were pleasant. Parents thanked the teachers for their contribution. One year, Vertus remembered, the parents and teachers collaborated on a harmless prank on Uncle Joe. Convincing him to arrive late one morning, his schedule was necessarily altered. When he arrived, he noticed a wagon and team of horses in the schoolyard and, at first, thought nothing of it. Some of the pupils were playing in the schoolyard as they usually did and greeted him as he started inside. When he opened the door, he was surprised to find all the parents were there. They had boards across their desks to be used as tables. Each was loaded with food. In the background everyone hollered, "Surprise!" Uncle Joe was speechless, and grateful.

The Ringworm Contamination

My next area of research led me to investigate the culprit central to this story, the ringworm outbreak. Ringworm could develop at any time and when it did, the disease was highly contagious. I discovered that the coatroom was the focal point for the outbreak, where the students at Lyles Station hung their garments. Head coverings were easily accessible and grabbed by students whenever exiting the building. Once break time ended, students would file back inside and return caps, jackets and other outerwear to any nail in the coatroom.

The actual classroom as it appeared in 1927 following restoration in year 2003. Above is a reenactment of days gone by, as schoolteacher Mary Madison brings children via fieldtrip to the replica classroom.

The efficient consolidation of outwear perhaps seems insignificant, until the possibility of a ringworm outbreak is considered. Ringworm is a highly contagious fungus that could leapfrog from garment to garment and easily spread in a coatroom of the kind at the Lyles Station School. It happened that sixteen students had contracted the disease.

Children are most susceptible to ringworm because of their close contact with each other. Melvin was one of the infected students who originally carried the disease home to Vertus. The brothers slept in the same bed, a rather common occurrence for families with multiple children; with ease, the fungus spread quickly among the brothers.

Traditionally ringworm forms a red, elevated, fast-spreading, ring-like sore on the skin. The center of the ring could be clear; however, the sore itself may be scaly, crusty, or fluid filled. Pain and itching sometimes accompany the lesions. Signs of the infection include reddening, scaling and blistering of the scalp with intense itching. Ringworm could appear as round or oval patches of baldness and can easily be confused with seborrhea or other known conditions.

Iodine was the most expedient remedy, available at the local drug store. The drug was not expensive and usually available in ample supply. It was a mainstay cure that shared place in earlier times medicine chests with other remedies like Bromo Seltzer and Castor Oil. Once applied on the ringworm fungus, it was just a matter of time before Iodine cured the infected area. The parents and children of Lyles Station would be introduced to the promise of a new, more modern treatment. It was first suggested to the school trustee, a Mr. Delong.

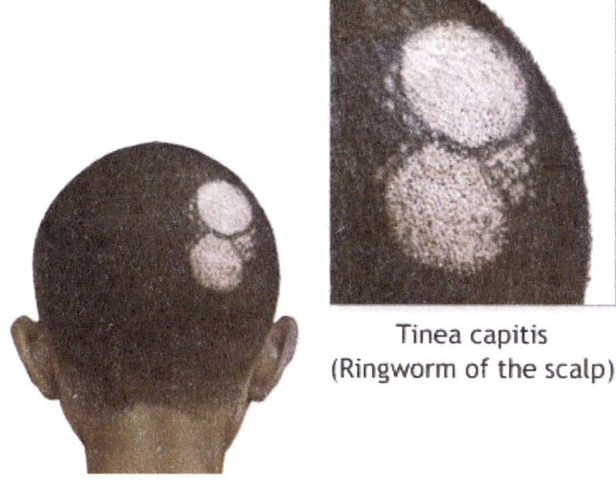

Tinea capitis (Ringworm of the scalp)

True to the style of the 1920s was the flat cap, similar to the one shown above. This cap was worn by the boys and hung on a nail in the school's coatroom.

"I believe in The Golden Rule: Do unto others, as you would wish them to do unto you."

-Vertus

Radiation Misunderstood

With my research trip only days away, I thought it best to better understand the cause for radiation testing and its role in Lyles Station. While one day questioning Vertus, I asked about his thoughts on radiation. He immediately said, "I don't like it. Just the mention of the word radiation strikes fear in me. Since the experiment, I have been afraid, never knowing what tomorrow might bring. I try to be optimistic in spite of the things I have read, things that describe destruction and even death to people over-exposed to radiation." He went on, "I do not want to think the worst, but I am terrified of developing cancer."

Vertus feared radiation and everything connected to it. He went to extremes to avoid it in any form and would not allow even the most common things into his home. He had no electronic gadgetry, particularly a microwave oven. He never owned a kitchen appliance outside a basic stove and refrigerator. Even the appliances he selected were plain as vanilla, without as much as a time clock. Vertus was terrified of any device capable of giving off radiation, no matter how small the potential dosage. For him, it was his unwavering rule, an unmistakable boundary between life and death.

I researched information that explained the popularity of radiation during 1927 and peered further into its development. I found that a German physicist named Wilhelm Roentgen discovered radiation in 1895, and it was initially greeted with wild enthusiasm. Over time its popularity gave way to alarm as unforeseen side effects appeared. The general public became cynical because of the lack of radiation protection standards.

Wilhelm Conrad Roentgen, photo from Encyclopedia Britannica

Roentgen invented radiation while working in his darkened laboratory and soon concluded that the new ray could pass through the tissue of humans, but not through their bones. His first experiment was a film displaying the hand of his wife, Bertha. He named the incredible glowing ray "X," for mystery. Never before had anyone seen a living human skeleton. Within months, hundreds of thousands of people were putting their hands, legs, or heads into the path of rays, and death followed, from exposure to the radiation emitted by the machines.

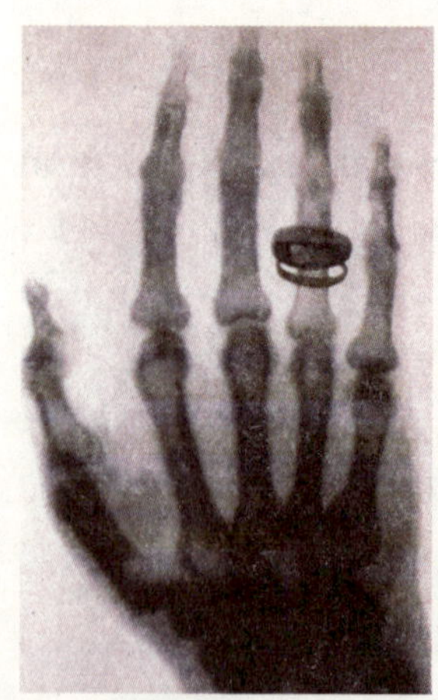

Two weeks following the discovery, X-ray images of Anna Bertha Roentgen's hand were taken on November 8th, 1895. When Anna saw her skeleton she exclaimed, "I have seen my death!"

Gibson County Hospital, where the experiments that affected the Lyles Station students took place, wanted to capitalize on the radiation mania gripping the country. Radiation was suggested to cure drunkards and smokers of addiction and to cure criminal behavior. By directing radioactive waves directly into the brain, radiation was suggested by doctors for treating headaches, acne, tonsils and adenoids. The hospital could earn even more by treating so-called female problems by irradiating a woman's ovaries to cure depression, or to bring about menopause.

The craze was so popular that people were willing to drink radium-based solutions, promoted as an all-purpose tonic to correct all ills. The drink was referred to as "liquid sunshine." There was plenty of money floating around and plenty of primitive machines with methods that exacerbated the danger of X-Ray in the early 1900's. Radiation became a commercialized, untested and out of control moneymaking scheme.

This was the problem that made its way to Lyles Station. It is believed that the local hospital acquired radiation machines and used Vertus and the other children from Lyles Station as specimens to learn how to best use it for treatment. Vertus stated, "They experimented on us to determine acceptable levels of tolerance that at the same time caused me the wound that I have today."

With this information in mind, I felt well enough informed and prepared to learn all I could while visiting Lyles Station, the town where it all began. As part of my plans, I wanted to meet descendants of those who founded the township, people Vertus spoke of with admiration. He once shared, "It was a black man who founded Lyles Station." Most importantly, I wanted to speak to the men and visit the sites where this horrible tragedy took place.

In 1932, an authoritative statement involving the dangers of drinking radioactive water or taking other medicines supposed to contain radium was issued by the American Medical Association stated, "There is absolutely no evidence that radium water is useful."

A Visit to Lyles Station

Finally, it came time for our visit to Lyles Station. We left during the summer of 2006. By then I knew most of Vertus' family history and his perspective on the experiment; however, no words can describe my thoughts of finally seeing the town firsthand and meeting the other survivors. I wanted to take photos of important landmarks and obtain detailed descriptions from the remaining victims. Vertus was understandably hesitant to revisit a dark time, seventy-nine years removed.

My particular interest was in seeing the old hospital where the experiments took place and the schoolhouse where the outbreak of ringworm occurred. I wanted to stand on the ground where Joshua Lyles dreamed of building the little township and learn more about the "Freedom Village." I was told that Lyles Station had historic ties to the routes traveled by escaped slaves, and I wanted to search for information about the Underground Railroad, popular during the mid-1800s.

Once we arrived, we immediately went to visit Vertus' brother Melvin, his cousins Melvin "Fuzz" and Horace, and his uncle Gletus. Each was in their late eighties, and they were all irradiated alongside Vertus. We were met with warm greetings, each hugging Vertus and me several times. They were filled with wholehearted excitement for this visit and discussion of the events of their childhood. These men were not what I expected, the street-fighter-vowing-to-wallop-any-person-responsible-for-their-injuries type. Instead they were forgiving men with deep attachments to their family, community, and faith.

The sign placed on Highway 64 directing visitors to Lyles Station.

For Vertus, the experience of this trip was very different. Returning to Indiana with a writer/producer there to record his story was both exciting and troubling. It was difficult for him because we were there to retrace a horrible memory. However, we both enjoyed a visit with Uncle Gletus, the youngest and only surviving brother of Vertus' deceased father, Claude. A mere two years older than Vertus, the two interacted more like brothers than uncle and nephew, but out of respect, Vertus always referred to him as uncle. Gletus welcomed Vertus and by the words they exchanged, I could tell they had not seen each other for some time.

Gletus was a farmer. He was a soft-spoken man who stood about 6 feet tall. He wore classic old time blue denim coveralls, always topped off with a kind of hat that resembled one worn by a railroad conductor. Gletus was born and raised in a house less than a mile from his present home. During a newspaper interview conducted in 2000, he was asked to what destination he would most like to travel. Gletus replied, "None." His family had farmed in Lyles Station for generations. In fact, his farm was one of the largest in Gibson County.

I later learned that Gletus, like Vertus, always paid his debts in full. One day while shopping for a tractor, he was ignored by most of the salesmen, possibly because he did not look the part of the well-to-do farmer. After an extended wait, Gletus asked for the manager and began to display his displeasure. Gletus then proceeded to order not one but two tractors, then pulled out his checkbook and wrote a check for the full purchase amount. Hopefully the salesmen that ignored him learned something that day.

Within minutes there was a knock at the door. Gletus answered and welcomed other members of the family. He then explained to me that there were two men named Melvin. One was Vertus' brother, and the other Vertus' first cousin, Melvin "Fuzz." Unfortunately, cousin Fuzz suffered a stroke and was confined to a nearby nursing home. We were scheduled to meet him the following day. It was Vertus' brother Melvin, and his cousin Horace who joined us.

During our conversation, the men thought I was Vertus' medical doctor. I smiled at their assumption and took the time to introduce myself. I told about my meeting Vertus' and our subsequent long friendship. I shared that with help from Vertus I had knowledge of their family tree and knew their Lyles Station history. Then, I sat back and listened to the men discuss old times. For an hour or so, I was a fly on the wall. I noticed they all wore hats and no one had hair atop their heads. Finally Vertus introduced me and explained to them why I wanted to tell their story.

I supported his statements, only inserting clarification when necessary. I explained that I wished to earn their trust and didn't want to be looked upon as some big shot movie producer type. Instead, I hoped to be seen as a person humbled while telling their incredible story. I wanted them to accept me as a younger brother type who happened to care deeply about what happened to them.

After sharing small talk and allowing Vertus the opportunity to catch up, I asked to begin taping and focused the discussion on the experiment. My first request was the toughest..."Could you each remove your hats and hairpieces?" I had no clue how they might respond, but it was Vertus who set the tone, the one with the worst situation of them all. Without hesitance he removed his beanie and dressing from atop his wound. When he did, they each seemed compelled to follow suit. Vertus had clearly suffered the most severe deformities. I then asked them to describe their feelings as they unveiled themselves, removing hats and wigs.

No one was comfortable…not even Vertus. Melvin replied, "I feel naked," while the others nodded in agreement. Only Vertus and Melvin wore wigs, all others chose hats. I heard confessions of shame, a constant companion that was prevalent most of their lives. They described how family and friends became protectors. And, yes, they remembered the bullies, though they were few. Melvin used the term disgrace. Remarkably, he added, "This is the first time I have ever taken my wig off in front of other people." Melvin always wore a toupee. He went on to say, "My son is fifty-eight years old and he has only seen my head a couple of times. Right now I really feel naked and very uncomfortable."

I noticed that each of the men presented a speckled scalp, some badly spotted amidst large pockets of lost skin color. Their skin was dry and scaly, microscopically thin in texture. Touching the scalp gave one the sensation of touching the skull bone directly. There was little cushion or elastic feeling to their skin.

When the men looked at Vertus, I could sense their fear that his was a predictor of their future. They asked questions of him and I listened attentively to his responses. Horace asked, "Did your head ever resemble mine then advance to that stage?" Vertus replied, "My head never looked like yours, my head always had terrible lesions and burning. Doctors told me I received more radiation than any case they ever witnessed." I felt the men were very concerned for Vertus while clearly understanding that Vertus' status was not necessarily a progression of their own.

Vertus and I were candid about all but one thing–neither one of us disclosed the just-learned diagnosis of cancer. We thought it would be best to share this piece of information later. One important question did surface by Gletus, "Could Vertus' condition advance to a terminal state?" At that point I had to be honest, I choked out the word, "Yes".

The discussion continued for many hours. In a small room in this small rural community, we talked and laughed like family. I was elated with the information and equally delighted with their kindness and generosity. Much from this conversation shaped the details of this story.

After a while, I thought it best to stop for the day. Vertus and I said our goodbyes and set up another meeting time and location to continue. The men hugged us again and expressed their gratitude for our visit. The mood was light and carefree. I could feel their genuine welcome and interest in helping me tell their story.

That evening, we rented a van and checked into a local hotel. Though Vertus was noticeably tired from traveling, he was excited to stay up and talk further. He said, "Wilbert, I never thought I would get back here for this kind of fellowship. There is no better way to come back home." Once settled in our room, I thought about the day's events and the stories I heard from the men. They reminded me of a song I heard during a visit to the Karaoke Lounge. It was a song recorded by Diana Ross entitled, *Good Morning Heartache*. The lyrics spoke of heartache, embarrassment and pain endured for a lifetime.

As I drifted to sleep, I reminisced about the heartache and pain the men must have faced only to awaken to find their wounds were still with them. That first night in Lyles Station, I hardly slept a wink, interrupted by the anticipation of the upcoming events.

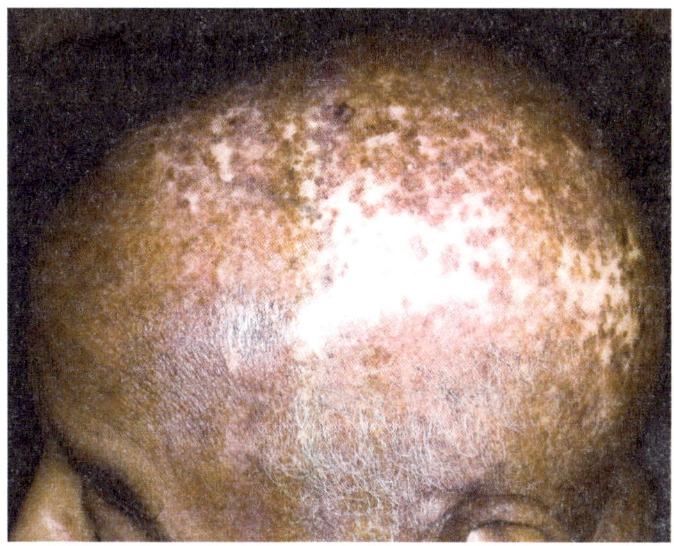

Above is the scalp of Horace Hardiman. Horace never wore a hairpiece but did wear a hat. Horace was one of the first treated and did not receive as much radiation as Vertus. (Photo 2006)

Horace Hardiman served in the U.S. Army 35 years before retiring.

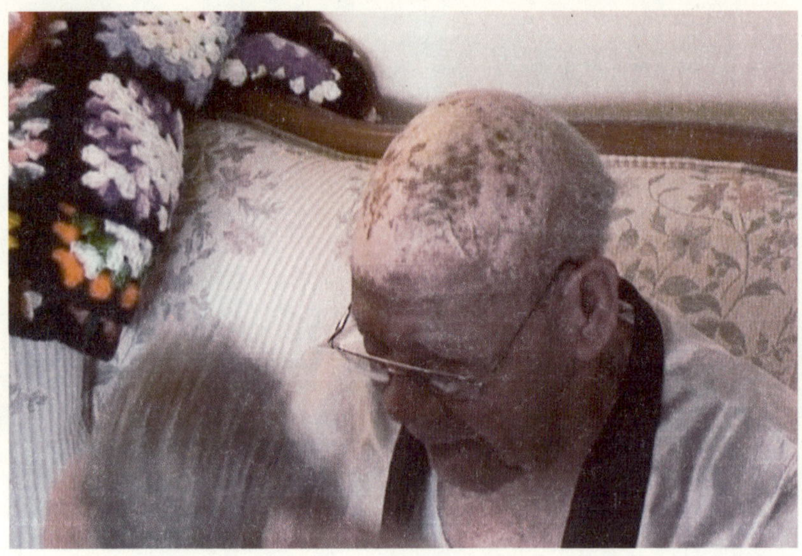

Melvin Hardiman takes his wig off for the first time publicly for this story. "I feel naked," describing the moment when he posed for a photo while removing his wig. Dependent on his cover, Melvin needed his hairpiece back on his head as quickly as possible. (Photo 2006)

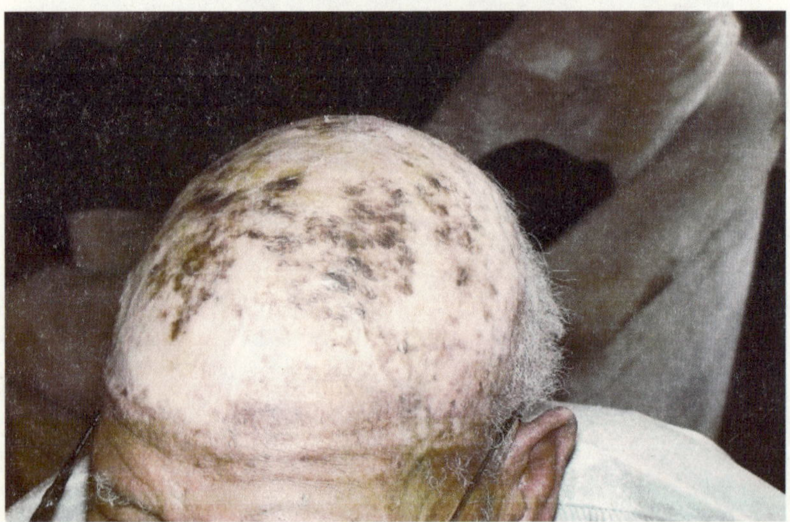

A closer look at Melvin's scalp as he stated, "This is the only photo of me ever taken without my hairpiece."

Melvin Hardiman, wearing one of the many hairpieces he wore over his lifetime. (Photo 1984)

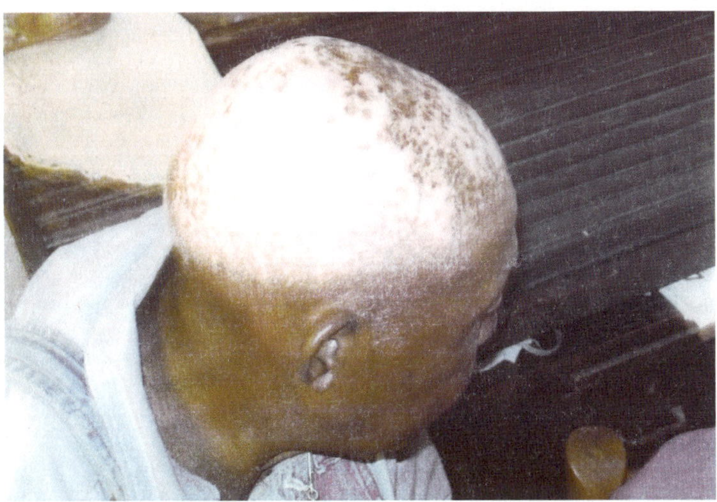

Gletus Hardiman was seven years old, a second grader in 1927. Like the others, he was affected by a simple case of ringworm that led to the experiments. Gletus never wore a wig but was seldom ever seen in public without a hat.

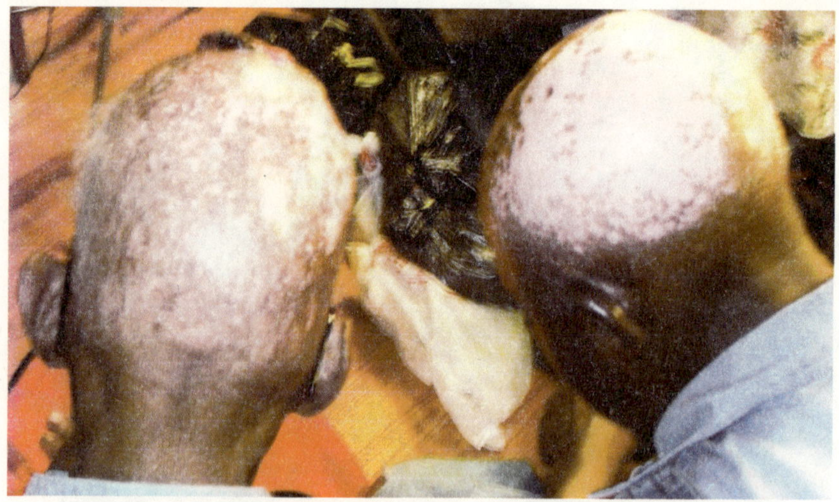

Vertus and Uncle Gletus pose together in 2006. If you look closely you might notice the effect of the oversized hat scarring their ears that in Vertus' case resulted in the ears becoming very thin. The men were completely bald with few traces of hair on their heads, however, their condition paled in comparison to that of Vertus.

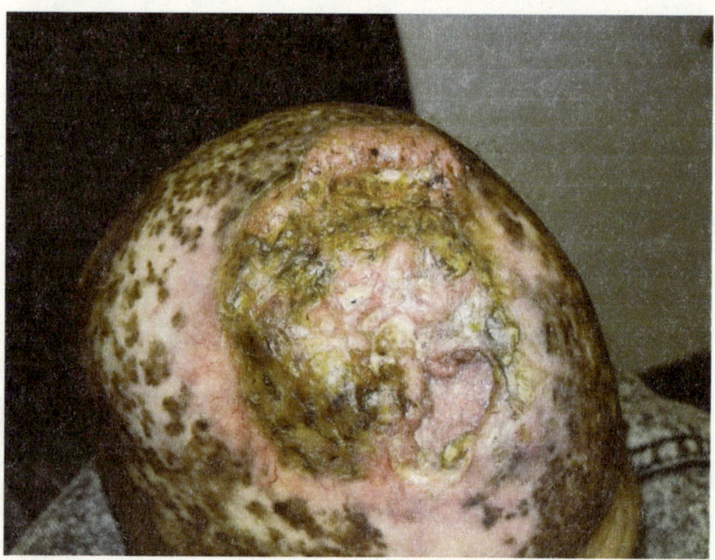

Vertus could no longer wear a wig due to the pain caused by its weight. This was the first time the other men saw Vertus' condition since 1936, when Vertus was a teenager. (Photo 2006)

Too Much Red Ink

Once we were together again, we returned to discussing the experiment. This time, I learned exactly how the perpetrators were able to carry out their plans. Together, the men explained how the situation unfolded with much clarity and precision. They remembered that the district school trustee was Mr. Delong, an appointee to the position. He faced no elections and therefore was only minimally accountable to parents who had no power to remove him through the ballot box. Trustee Delong oversaw education for the Patoka Township, Gibson County, Indiana, that included the unincorporated settlement at Lyles Station.

Uncle Joe shared with his family the fact that Trustee Delong would question him about his educational techniques, and the subsequent superior results. When Lyles Station academic achievement was compared to local white schools, Lyles Station students consistently proved something magical, superior academic achievement. The students scored consistently among the best in the state, making Uncle Joe an easy target of watchfulness.

Trustee Delong had a brother-in-law, Dr. Ellis from nearby Mt. Carmel. Ellis served as head physician at the county sanitarium (hospital). The two were considered workaholics, very friendly to each other.

The sanitarium was constructed in 1905. Three local doctors conceived the idea of opening a sanitarium, and then, finally, in 1907, at a cost of 30,000 dollars, the three-story structure with a basement was completed. The local media identified the sanitarium as having facilities well ahead of its time. It would primarily serve the white community of Gibson County and was situated four miles east of

Lyles Station.

The sanitarium gained a reputation of operating in the red, never turning a profit. In 1910, a mere three years following the arrival of its first patient, the facility was forced to close its doors. The Princeton Daily Democrat reported the event in the following headline: "*Princeton Sanitarium Is Closed, Nurses Left The City, Sanitarium Closed Its Doors.*" The community responded with anger, some taking it upon themselves to open their homes to medical services. One prominent home was operated just blocks from the original sanitarium.

The sanitarium remained closed for years and the local Lyles Station midwife saw to most of the Negro community's medical needs. There were numerous attempts to purchase the hospital first in 1912, then again in 1915, before a valid purchase was finalized in 1917. The facility reopened as County Methodist Episcopal Hospital. The purchase price was 20,000 dollars. Perhaps a better financial future was on the horizon.

It is believed that Delong and Ellis collaborated on ways to address the hospital's financial dilemma. They more than likely knew each other's environment well—Ellis aware of the ringworm outbreak and Delong of the hospital's financial condition. Marginal income continued to trickle in, creating the need for greater revenue sources. As an integral part of management, Dr. Ellis represented the hospital as a senior medical voice and goodwill ambassador within Gibson County.

During this time, the media identified the radiation craze sweeping the United States, and institutions across the country, including Gibson General, were well aware of the new invention. Everyone sought a piece of the cash cow. Gibson General was no exception. The hospital received a gift of radiation equipment, but it fell into untrained hands. They developed a plan to get their training through experiments on children from Lyles Station. Trustee Delong offered the students as an ideal strategy.

Dr. Ellis needed practice to understand human tolerance of radiation, that is, how to set the dials for safe levels. He needed to train technicians to deliver applications of radiation to whites. He cleverly gained access to the Negro children at Lyles Station, who would be used as guinea pigs. Parents would be coerced into signing a field trip permission slip that would in itself, serve as tacit approval to conduct the treatment. Experimental training at Gibson General would demand that ten children would become victims.

For Dr. Ellis, the children of Lyles Station were a firsthand account of the effects of overexposure. The ringworm infection was the perfect target disease, seldom limited to a single case because it was so contagious. They knew it would easily spread and any outbreak would mean an ample supply of test subjects.

Gibson County Sanitarium as it was first known, was built in 1906, photo provided by Gibson General hospital.

A hospital rededication in 1917 established the hospital name as County Methodist Episcopal Hospital before later being referred to as Gibson General Hospital.

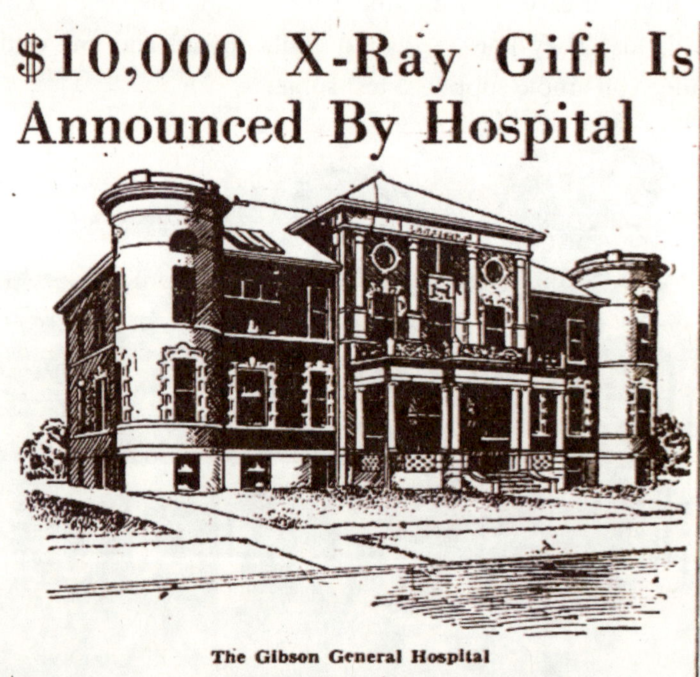

$10,000 X-Ray Gift Is Announced By Hospital

The Gibson General Hospital

News article recognizing the generous gift made from the estate of a prominent local family.

Within A Dungeon

Further discussion and research revealed that Delong later contacted Uncle Joe to get the latest count of students affected with ringworm. One could assume he needed to work quickly before the drug iodine had time to cure the fungus. Uncle Joe provided a count of sixteen cases. The trip to the hospital was planned and the permission slips were drawn for parent approval.

The hospital advertised the experiment as a new and innovative cure for ringworm, a message to be communicated to each parent. Delong was designated to deliver the message personally. These men were about to play with the lives of innocent children, in the end affecting their long-term health. The hospital was looking for financial gain, a dollar here and there. But for the children recruited, the experimental treatments would mean a daily appointment with misery and pain for the remainder of their lives.

There were cases of children with ringworm all over the county, but the Lyles Station children were targeted. Parents expected Uncle Joe to be knowledgeable of any so-called new procedure and trusted his judgment, assuming he was fine with the proposed new treatment. The Hardiman men stated, "Our parents assumed that if Uncle Joe was a part of it, then it must be okay." After all, the majority of the children affected with the ringworm were Hardimans, Uncle Joe's nieces and nephews. But Delong kept the school principal totally in the dark. Uncle Joe knew nothing about the plot.

Delong personally spoke with eight families. Some had more than one child affected. Perhaps his goal was to obtain the needed signatures on permission slips, signatures that would authorize travel to the hospital and subsequent treatment of the children. Many recounted the story about these visits and remember that Delong was very brief and never uttered the word radiation. Vertus said, "Delong made it appear as though this treatment was reserved previously for white children only, and through his efforts, approval had been won for application on Negroes." None of this was true. Vertus went on to say, "Delong threatened school closure if the fungus was not eradicated."

The story of a new procedure did not sit well with the Greer family, who did not give their permission for the treatment. They elected to treat their child's ringworm by applying a copper penny, dipped in vinegar, to the affected area. This treatment was successful in healing their family member without any scarring.

On the contrary, others may have consented to save on the purchase of iodine or lye soap, both common cures for ringworm. The prospect of free medical care was enticing. But the families would soon realize these glittering promises did not translate into golden opportunity. Ultimately, permission was granted to treat ten children on Wednesday, December 14, 1927.

Vertus was a part of the experiment by pure happenstance. There was no grade called kindergarten; school began at first grade when a student was age six. Vertus was only five. Irene elected to send Vertus to school along with Melvin to receive the so-called innovative medical treatment. For Vertus this day was not a normal first day experience; it was memorable, but for all the wrong reasons. In essence he would come to associate school with torture.

On Wednesday morning Irene walked her sons out to the Highway 64 bus stop, then gave her boys a morning farewell. Her final words to her boys were, "Melvin you take care of your little brother." She had no idea that when she would next see her sons, their condition would be very different.

Vertus recalled his mixed emotions. He was excited about going to school with his brother, but he was also afraid of the treatment. Vertus told me, "It helped me to see the other kids on the bus and the thought of some of them also getting the treatment eased my fears."

The school bus was an old Dodge with a STOP sign positioned just outside the driver-side window. The bus fit three children per seat, with a maximum capacity of approximately 25 students. Mr. Clift drove the school bus. He was married to Vertus' aunt and had driven the Lyles Station route for thirty-seven years. Mr. Clift was rumored to have missed only one day of service, and that due to the passing of his mother.

One by one, children from grades one through eight entered the bus. Young boys wore flat caps, winter jackets and overcoats. Ankle length dresses; sweaters and coats adorned young females. When the bus finally arrived at school, approximately 24 students exited. This part was all so new and exciting for Vertus. He still clung close to Melvin. He saw kids frolicking on the school's acre of grass. Routinely the bus arrived ten to fifteen minutes early, providing the children time for a game of jacks, marbles or the like.

Finally Uncle Joe appeared, standing erect on the front porch. This alerted the children that it was time for school to begin. Uncle Joe was a no-nonsense disciplinarian and as a result, like little soldiers, his students quietly filed into the schoolhouse.

J. Leslie (Les) Clift. Mr. Clift drove the Lyles route from 1922 to 1958. He died August 15, 1964, the result of an auto accident. (Photo 1927)

The children with ringworm were instructed to wait at the front entrance. A head cover applied by Mr. Clift made them easy to identify. Within minutes, nine students, eight boys and one girl joined Vertus. Mr. Clift went in to see Uncle Joe who gave him last minute instruction. He told Mr. Clift that the children were assigned to see Dr. Ellis and the treatment should not take very long. Uncle Joe knew the children were nervous and chose to gather them around. He knelt down to provide eye contact while informing Vertus and the others that the ringworm infection would soon go away.

The children walked single file to the waiting bus. Vertus drifted towards the back showing little interest in this part of the adventure. Melvin remained by his side as the children boarded.

The atmosphere on the bus was intense. Mr. Clift attempted to divert attention by singing a school song, but the children showed little interest. Silence gripped the air. He decided to leave well enough alone and refocused his attention on driving. The sound of the old four-cylinder engine lumbering down the road is a sound Vertus recalls even today. He sat snuggled against Melvin, each taking comfort from the other. Within minutes they arrived at the hospital. The time was approximately 8:47 am.

Mr. Clift was forty-five years old, old enough to be familiar with segregation and its related ugliness. He knew the lawful procedure associated with the county hospital where Negros could not park anywhere on the grounds and were required to enter through the rear door. However, on this day Mr. Clift followed instructions to drive the children onto the premises and parked the bus near the rear entry. Historically, rain, snow, injury or even near death conditions could not serve as a valid reason to violate the segregation laws. This day was different.

The door of the bus opened and one by one the children exited. They followed Mr. Clift, engaging in a slow walk towards the entrance. They were trembling noticeably. Vertus continued to bring up the rear staying close to his brother. Mr. Clift urged the children not to worry and guaranteed them all would be fine. He wanted the children to trust him. Mr. Clift and Uncle Joe did not realize they were part of a larger plot to deliver children posthaste to a laboratory housed within a dungeon.

Inside the hospital, they walked down a short flight of stairs into the basement. The children were in a strange land proceeding as though prisoners in route to the gallows. At the end of the path stood a waiting Dr. Ellis, a tall man who seemed to tower over the children. He was age sixty or so, and wore a knee-length white coat.

He offered no greeting and acted very abruptly. He was the complete opposite of the more nurturing Mr. Clift. There were no balloons or coloring books distributed and no welcome committee to interact with the children. The basement's temperature was as could be expected, uncomfortably chilling.

Communication with the children was very limited, primarily reserved for direction and restricting movement. Commands, such as line-up, wait here, stand up or sit down were the order. The children were treated more as specimens and not patients. Dr. Ellis suggested to Mr. Clift that the wait might be lengthy and subsequently directed him to wait on the bus. This seemed a bit odd because Uncle Joe did not infer that the trip would require Mr. Clift to remain at the hospital for very long. There was an expectation of minimal instructional time lost.

Not thinking much of it and seeing nothing wrong, Mr. Clift assumed the hospital had their best interest at heart. He turned towards the children, knelt down and stated, "These nice people are going to do something to make those awful ringworms go away. It won't hurt." The children nodded in the affirmative, then reluctantly turned and watched Mr. Clift exit the door.

Now in total control, Dr. Ellis led the children through the basement corridor into a small room. He was quickly accompanied by three young technicians, each appeared in their mid twenties. They also wore white lab coats, and each was there to fill a particular role. There was limited time for the experiment, given that Uncle Joe expected the children to return within a reasonable amount of time.

The first technician was assigned the responsibility of corralling the children in the hallway, subsequently sending them, when requested, into the treatment room. The second technician manned the equipment controls, dispensing previously determined levels of radiation, prescribed by Dr. Ellis. The radiation dosage would become progressively stronger with each child. The ninth child treated, Melvin, was to have less radiation than Vertus, the last (tenth) to be treated. The question remained—how much radiation is too much?

The third technician was assigned to accompany Dr. Ellis during the observation and evaluation phase. This was the room where effects could be measured. The goal was to best understand tolerable volumes by exploring the outer boundaries of radiation safety.

One technician sat in a chair directing the children as needed into the treatment room. The children were instructed to sit on the floor, single file, along the hallway wall with their legs closed. They were taken one at a time for this experiment and their sequence was by coincidence. The child at the end of the line was conceivably the youngest and most frightened; this fitting description represented the young and timid Vertus, fearing what would happen to him on his very first day of school.

We stopped taping for the day. Vertus needed to change his dressing and the hour was late. Later that night, I recalled information I had discovered during my research at home. I noticed information on Vertus' birth certificate and found it ironic, and difficult to believe, that Dr. Ellis was the birthing physician whose signature appeared on Vertus' birth certificate. Could it be true that the same doctor who signed Vertus' record of life could be the same person who performed a life altering experiment? Could Ellis become such an instrument of pain, guilty of such an appalling misdeed?

When viewing Vertus' birth certificate, the following words are so noted and signed by Dr. Ellis. This document was completed and signed by Dr. Ellis on March 13, 1922.

I hereby certify that I attended the birth of this child, who was born alive at 2:20 am, on March 9, 1922, signed by, W.L. Ellis, Attending Physician, and County M.E. Hospital, at Princeton Indiana.

I had to pause for a moment, thinking back to this discovery. Amazed at this story, my mind took me back to a Karaoke performance weeks past. A lady sang the song *Heatwave*, originally performed by Martha and the Vandellas. I was reminded of the description Vertus used to depict the burning sensation in his head and scalp. He described the burning in this way; "It is as though you place your hand on a hot stove top." I asked more about it and Vertus told me he would explain it in greater detail later. Like the words of the song, I could only imagine Vertus feeling a *heatwave*.

RESTRAINED AND POISONED

If there had ever been a time when I felt most awkward, it was during the discussions I had with the men over the course of our next conversations. I vividly recall their body language and the way they shifted forward to sit on the edge of their chairs while they shared their troubling accounts. I recall the change in their posture, the way they sat with their shoulders drooping downward, while looking down at the floor. Their hands were positioned to cradle their heads. The subject at hand was recounting the events in the basement.

The air in the room thickened as their anxiety rose. The men described their pain and fear, more frightened by the moment. It was as if the horrible event was being relived with each word they spoke. Yet with remarkable strength, the men began to recount the events in chorus, as if reading from the same page of the same script.

One of the men stated, "They blasted us, it seemed to go on forever." While another said, "I am shivering as I remember that day, while so many of you are present here with me." They mentioned hearing shouts, screams, squirming and kicking. Vertus said, "They didn't care." Another added, "My palms are wet as we talk about this, 80 years later." One added, "I'm sure that technician who pulled the lever had feelings for her loved ones, but one thing for sure, that day she had no concern for us kids." He went on to say, "This is the first time we have come together to talk about this with anyone."

Horace recalled, "I was so scared and hurting so that I could hardly breathe...I remember being dizzy and burning so badly. I didn't know who those people were or why they caused us such pain." Today they each believed that Dr. Ellis was not interested in curing ringworm. Instead his only concern seemed to be their reaction to the radiation.

I asked if anyone could remember how long he was forced to endure the radiation. "How long did the experiment last?" No one remembered exactly, but Vertus did say "We were in so much agony; we couldn't measure it in time. Even a minute may not seem very long until you draw a comparison. Imagine your scalp held to a hot stove for just two seconds...then reconsider the span of a minute."

The men went on to speak for themselves, their parents, and uncles Joe and Les Clift. Their stories joined, unifying, as they each retold their version. Sequentially, where one man stopped, the other would chime in, adding details and pertinent information. With enthusiasm, they shared their story.

First, each child was placed in the treatment chair. While there, they were told to sit atop books to ensure their head would clear the backrest. Next, each child's arms were strapped to the chair armrest to restrict movement. Once secured, the technician placed a hat-like device on the victim's head; it was white in color with purple striping. Electrical wires were attached to the device that joined the child to a nearby machine. Each of the children was subjected to full-body radiation, absorbed directly through their head.

The head covering used was many sizes too large and flopped down to cover most of the children's forehead. It came to rest just above the eyebrows and covered a portion of their ears. Then the technician ordered each child, "Don't move" before throwing a switch.

Once the experiment concluded, the child was led in their hysterical state to a final room. There, a third technician assisted Dr. Ellis who observed their outcomes. The plan seemed to be working perfectly. It was assumed that Dr. Ellis was looking for signs of scalp burn, hair loss, drowsiness and other ailments.

There was a screen designed to safeguard the technician. It was difficult to imagine the safety precaution they took compared to the reckless disregard for the wellbeing of the children.

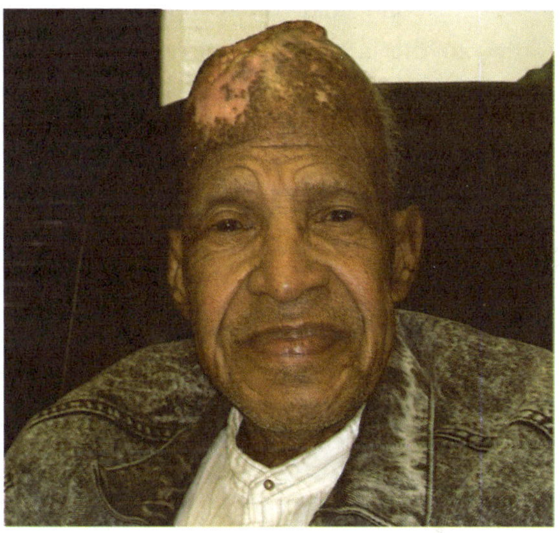

Notice the outline of the cover placed upon Vertus' head during the experiment. It burned a permanent scar around the circumference of his head. Look closer to view the burning of the upper portion of his left ear that was left wafer thin by the radiation.

Dr. Ellis heard the children complain of severe scalp burning, dizziness and headaches. The symptoms were identical for each child. The doctor told the kids it would be ok, that the pain was temporary and would go away at any moment. They heard Ellis dismiss their complaints as minor, but in reality the kids were fairing far worse than he had anticipated. Their poor condition did not stop the experiments.

The children pleaded for relief from the burning but Ellis only responded with the promise that the hurting would soon go away. In reality, Ellis seemed to have no knowledge of how to treat the damage inflicted on these children, or whether they would be permanently injured. The children's pain did not subside. It intensified.

Vertus told that he was the last to enter. He stated, "They told me to sit in a high back wooden chair on top of some books, then they strapped my arms to the chair." They turned the radio's volume to maximum capacity. Everyone remembered the radio that rested on a shelf in the radiation room. It became a symbol of their pain. The music played loudly to muffle any screams. Perhaps most important, it stifled any warning to those not yet treated, a precursor to their pending fate. This was a far cry from the sterile environment hospitals are generally known for. On that long ago day in the Gibson General Hospital, these children experienced something very different.

The room was no larger than the size of a large storage closet about eight-by-six feet in diameter. There were no ornaments hanging on its walls.

By now the oversized hat-like device was placed on Vertus' head. He slammed his eyelids shut, as he heard the command "Don't move." Vertus said, "I was shaking so hard, I was so scared." Vertus began to cry as he continued, "I felt so much heat all over my body that got stronger. Then, I remember my head was ringing." I surmised that his small body was screaming with alarm, revolting against the intrusion of radiation.

The heat quickly grew. Vertus said, "I screamed as loud as I could." Unfortunately his screams were not heard, drowned out by music playing at maximum volume. Vertus continued, "I stretched my legs as far forward as I possibly could as if by some small miracle, I could reach the floor." But, unfortunately, there was no escape.

When the machine was mercifully turned off the technician reentered the room. The men remembered the foul smell in the air, the result of their burning hair and flesh. The technician removed the head cover, looked down at Vertus and was startled. She reacted frantically saying, "Oh my God, I've given him (Vertus) too much."

As Vertus recalls the moment, he again cried. The other men in the interview were noticeably touched, their eyes also tearing. Together, this family shared their emotions. Vertus spoke, "I was petrified. I have never been more afraid at any other point in my life."

Vertus continued the story, "I continued to scream while still restrained." The technician reacted by bolting through the door to find Dr. Ellis. In her haste she failed to close the door behind her. The children who were already treated could hear the radio, but they also heard the even louder screams from Vertus. This exacerbated an already intense situation. Chaos erupted. The technician relayed to Dr. Ellis what she had done, and the men remembered seeing Ellis hurry to Vertus' side.

Fearing the worst for his brother, Melvin said, "I ran as fast as I could to find Mr. Clift." Maybe he was the only person capable of rescuing them from this horrible situation. Melvin flung open the rear door of the hospital and instantaneously began to pound his fist at the bus door. With a burst of excitement and fear, Melvin shouted, "Mr. Clift, Mr. Clift, come quick, they're hurting Vertus!"

Melvin said, "Mr. Clift was startled, just shaken from a nap." The disbelieving sight of Melvin startled him. He jerked the handle forward as abruptly as he could to open the door. Melvin was heaving and in the midst of an uncontrollable vomit. Mr. Clift was quick to react and speechless, singularly driven to ensure that the other children were safe. Melvin dropped to his knees with exhaustion ordered by Mr. Clift, "Wait by the bus. I'll be right back.

I'll be right back."

Mr. Clift burst through the door in search of the children, as Melvin explained. He assumed the children were somewhere in the basement but was frightened by the prospect of tragedy. The sight of Melvin triggered the question for him: what are they doing to the children? He knew something was not right with Melvin. Something made him appear very sick. Perhaps the other children were suffering an equal or worse fate. He needed to find them quickly, especially Vertus, the youngest boy in the group, who was, he would come to find, injured worse than all.

While he located the children, some were standing, bent over in response to their pain. Some lay on the floor, one in the fetal position. No matter what their level of pain, once they heard Mr. Clift, they tried somehow to attach themselves to him. They were in obvious pain, in a real bad state. Mr. Clift was furious.

Once through the door, he spotted the technician that assisted Dr. Ellis during the observation phase. "Where is the doctor?" Mr. Clift shouted. The technician was so startled and quickly may have concluded that this was becoming more than he signed on for. He pointed Mr. Clift towards the treatment room. The children somehow managed to follow Mr. Clift. Moving through the halls, he frantically shouted, "Vert-tus!"

Vertus heard him and reacted, screaming even louder. Dr. Ellis was at Vertus' side, attempting to calm him and render aide. As Dr. Ellis struggled nervously to release the restraints, Mr. Clift overtook him and attempted to lift Vertus from the chair. It was obvious that he was severely over-exposed to the radiation. Vertus was hysterical and appeared unable to walk. Through the chaos everyone shouted because the music was still turned to maximum volume. Elkin's begged for time to treat Vertus and the others; he felt he could not let the children leave in their current state.

Mr. Clift was furious, and refused Elkin's requests. The men said that Mr. Clift questioned himself and his decision to leave them alone with Ellis. He knew they needed immediate care and felt he was their only hope of rescue. He wanted the children out of the hospital and home where they could receive it. But he would quickly realize that it would be difficult to treat the children because they did not know what they were fighting.

At this time, no one, outside of Delong and Ellis, knew the children were just given radiation and it would be sometime before the truth would surface.

The technician assisting with the observations apparently experienced a change of heart. In a complete reversal, he became a caregiver. He assisted Mr. Clift. He scooped up Vertus and urged Mr. Clift to lead the way. The young man was in good physical condition compared to the older Mr. Clift, who welcomed the help. This was the same technician who seemed so heartless earlier. The severity of Vertus' condition was greatly noticeable, leading to his change of heart.

Mr. Clift brought the children aboard the bus while the technician, arms wrapped around Vertus, placed him aboard in the seat just behind the driver. Mr. Clift had no clue what he was dealing with and no idea what had taken place inside the hospital. Moving as fast as he could, he ran outside to the bus' hood and frantically turned the engine's crank. There standing in his way was Dr. Ellis, with whom Mr. Clift wanted nothing to do. He pushed him aside and closed the bus door behind him.

Mr. Clift shouted at the kids, "What did they do to you in there?" There was no answer, each student was helplessly confused and in pain. He jumped into the driver's seat with one eye on his disheveled passengers and the other careful not to injure Dr. Ellis who was still pleading for a moment with the children, positioning himself just outside the driver's side window, "I can help them," shouted Ellis. But his urging was completely ignored. Mr. Clift shouted the question as he began to drive forward, "What did you do to them?" The only response was a faint voice heard from a child, "They burned us with that thing." The voice was that of Melvin who cried huge tears. Melvin shared the seat with Vertus who laid his head across Melvin's lap.

Mr. Clift pushed the old bus to its limits. He was careful not to overturn or meet with an unfortunate mishap. He looked down at his uniform and could see hair clinging to it—hair that was once worn by the children, uprooted by radiation. The stench of urine and fecal matter was also obvious, detected on most of the children. After driving for only a minute, the children were jostled in response to the unpaved roads. The erratic motion led most of the children to vomit uncontrollably, heaving in every corner of the bus. In almost chain-like reaction, the children were gagging loudly and had extreme fits of diarrhea as well.

Mr. Clift wondered where to go for help. The very hospital charged with the responsibility of curing patients is the one responsible for this problem. Mr. Clift tried to make sense of this. His main question remained, "What happened back there?" Now, Melvin was again vomiting. One thing was certain; of all the children on board, Vertus was the most seriously injured. He left the hospital carrying the greatest amount of radiation. At five-years-old, Vertus had faced the event that would have the greatest physical impact on his 85 years of life.

We concluded the discussions for the day, though no one wanted to stop talking. The men spoke with determination and force as if I were a judge and they were pleading their case in a courtroom for the first time. We had talked for hours and I insisted that we stop and resume tomorrow. Hesitantly, they obliged.

"If I am angry then my heart's not right and my prayers would not be answered."

-Vertus

Ringing the Bell

The next day the men started talking with the same enthusiasm. They spoke fast, and sat at the edge of their chairs, as if they had to hurry and get their story out before someone might cut them off. Melvin said, "Wilbert you just don't know. I couldn't sleep last night thinking about so much that I want to say." The others nodded in agreement.

So we continued. They picked up right where the story left off. The first stop was the home of Henry and Ora Mae Hardiman. Their four sons, Garwood, Horace, Melvin "Fuzz" and Lloyd were onboard. As misfortune would have it, forty percent of the children treated belonged to this one family. Ora later stated that she remembered hanging the wash while Henry was tending the crops.

Mr. Clift drove the length of the driveway, stopping near the front porch. He sounded the horn as he approached in hopes of gaining assistance. He jumped out and pounded on the door. As he knocked, he peered through the sheer patterned curtains while shouting, "Ora, Henry, are you home?" Ora opened the door and Mr. Clift summoned her toward the bus. Ora was staggered by what she saw. She ran out past the bus directly to the distress bell to summon Henry from the fields. During that time Mr. Clift carried Lloyd into the house and laid him on the sofa and returned to get his brother, Melvin "Fuzz."

By the time Ora returned, her other two boys Horace and Garwood were walking, assisted by Mr. Clift. Ora frantically questioned Mr. Clift, but he had no time for discussion. Ora grabbed her boys; saw their blisters and the resulting burns. Mr. Clift had no answers, no answers at all! Ora rushed back to the distress bell, located just off the rear porch. Assuming an awful fiery accident had befallen her sons, she was now frantically ringing the bell. This was not one son ill—it was all four.

The distress bell is an old-fashioned field tradition that predates the telephone. A family member signaled others working in the field that a meal was ready by ringing the bell. A faster, more frantic ring usually signaled greater urgency or an emergency.

All Mr. Clift could tell Ora was, “Something is wrong with them, I’ve got others on the bus that are just as sick that I must take home. I’ve got to go.” As Mr. Clift backed down the driveway, he saw Henry running towards the house.

Mr. Clift later told his family about the event and how he realized that after what he witnessed with Ora Hardiman, he knew his remaining deliveries would be just as, or even more stressful. The questions he most feared were those that were likely to come when the parents learned he was on the bus the entire time and not with the children. The families were certain to demand answers.

The bus entered the Stewart farm next. Mr. Clift drove down the extremely long driveway, which, in this case, spanned the length of a football field. He honked the horn repeatedly during his approach hoping the Stewarts would emerge. Young Milburn was unable to walk unassisted, no doubt dizzy and nauseous. Livola Stewart peered out the window, immediately sensing danger. Consequently, her penetrating and panic-stricken voice cried out her inquiries.

“What happened to Milburn?” she asked. “I don’t know,” replied Mr. Clift. “All I know is that the hospital did it… all the kids I took there are now real sick.” Livola later stated that Mr. Clift looked back over his shoulder at her, with tears flowing from his eyes and stated, “They did something real bad to those kids. They hurt ‘em real bad!”

He told her that he had others to take home and there was no time to talk. Livola asserted that she was not satisfied, and in a stern voice she demanded an explanation. "What did they do to my boy?" Mr. Clift had to go, and he did so. As he backed down the driveway, he could hear her rapidly ringing the bell, hoping to summons her husband Wayman.

He traveled next to the home of Vertus and Melvin Hardiman. Mr. Clift had not paused long enough to evaluate any of the children, especially Vertus. The boy was lying on the seat in his own vomit absorbed by a web of nervous trembles. As Mr. Clift lifted Vertus, the stains on the front and backside of his clothing were noticeable. His hair was completely singed. Vertus was really sick, in desperate need of medical attention. Melvin stood on his own, which freed Mr. Clift to carry Vertus.

Melvin, recalling the incident, added, "Mr. Clift moved as fast as he could. As he approached the porch he began pounding on the front door, in a completely exhausted state." During the seconds before the door opened he pondered what to tell Claude and Irene. How could he explain something that he had no real knowledge about? He knew he must remain focused to get in and out quickly for the sake of those remaining on the bus.

Immediately Irene opened the door and said, "Lord, I knew better than to trust that Delong." She was just like the other parents, unsure of what to do or how to begin to help her children. Melvin remembered that she was screaming and during her haste went to find Claude. Mr. Clift turned to leave, but not before pledging to return to check on the children.

Mr. Clift retreated to the bus leaving Irene to take her anger out on the distress bell, clanging a sound to tell of frustration and mystery, similar to the families before her.

The next stop was the home of students Ella Mae and Allen Hardiman. Ella was the only girl treated. The sight of her hair falling out by the handful was not easy to take in. She was badly burned and continued to vomit. As a little girl, she was afforded no special treatment; as all were, she was fair game for Ellis' experiments. Both she and Allen were very sick and unable to walk on their own.

Mr. Clift reported that he drove to the entrance to the house and parked as close to the front door as he could. He turned and spoke to his passengers, "Ella, Allen, you're home," but apparently the two did not respond. He shook them but they were unable to rise upon their feet. He struck the buses' horn while simultaneously shouting, "Frank, Oma!" Exhausted, he hadn't any more strength to carry the children, but he would if necessary. He first grabbed Ella and went to the door.

Unfortunately there was no response. He went to the rear door in hopes of spotting someone, but there was still no answer. Mr. Clift ran to the rear and began ringing the distress bell, but Oma and Frank Hardiman were nowhere to be found. Another bell could be heard in the distance still ringing from the tragedy. The bells began to alert the entire community.

Frank and Oma were away, in route to help their neighbor in response to their bell. They had no knowledge of the urgency that had befallen their own children. Mr. Clift was faced with a major dilemma…what to do with Ella and Allen? Where can he take them? He placed them back on the bus and drove to the home of Gletus Hardiman.

Mr. Clift arrived at the home of James and Luella Hardiman, Gletus' parents. Gletus was two years older than Vertus and the youngest brother of Vertus' father Claude. James and Luella were both home. They were very willing to nurture their son Gletus and temporarily take charge of the care for their niece and nephew. They were similarly traumatized and outwardly fuming, predictably asking a number of questions. The children were listless and still vomiting, unable to hold down the contents of their stomach. At this time, Mr. Clift felt crushed under the pressure of all he had faced, and needed to retreat. He walked out the door and boarded the bus.

The men recalled Mr. Clift's description of the bus. He referred to it as a scene of horror and a reminder that something went terribly wrong. He drove down the road a short distance and pulled off to the side of the road to gather his thoughts. He could hear the children's cries, a reverberation in his subconscious mind. He thought, "I left them alone with Ellis." He then became tormented by the question—what could they do to the children to cause such a reaction?

Mr. Clift recalled that he was so "dog-tired" that every fabric in his body called for rest. They said that he cried with a single thought in mind; he had to get midwife Annie Mae James to help somehow. He would soon learn that she was contacted and already in route to one of the families. His next thought was to dread returning to the school. Did Uncle Joe know anything about this? Mr. Clift would later learn that he and Uncle Joe were both taken in by the hidden agenda of Ellis and Delong, men who were supposed to have been trustworthy.

The bus began to run hot, steam streaming from the radiator cap. The old bus mirrored Mr. Clift's exhaustion. He continued to drive, slowly, making his way back to the school; while, in the distance, the sound of a single distress bell still rang.

Vertus and Gletus Hardiman exchange stories about the distress bell mounted just outside the rear door of the farmhouse once owned by James and Luella Hardiman. The bell is an old-fashioned field tradition that pre-dates the telephone. It was used to signal those working the field that a meal was ready. A faster, more frantic paced ring usually meant an emergency.

THE BLAME GAME

Deflated, the men continued to share their story. They recalled information with a frustrated and saddened tone. They shared that Mr. Clift returned to the school, parking the bus a distance from its normal spot before discretely entering the building. Uncle Joe was in a classroom teaching. Mr. Clift surprised him when he cracked the classroom door and whispered, summoning him to the hallway. Given his outward appearance and unpleasant odor, it was easy to detect that something had gone wrong. Uncle Joe reacted fearfully, thinking that an unfortunate accident had taken place. He asked about the whereabouts of the children and what went wrong?

Marguerite Russell Johnson, now age 94, was 10 years old and a student in Uncle Joe's class the morning of the experiments. She said, "We were afraid that morning of the treatments. We (students) were so close and loved one another dearly. My desk was nearest the door when Mr. Clift called Uncle Joe. Uncle Joe stepped outside the classroom for a short time then returned to say he had to leave."

Uncle Joe took Mr. Clift downstairs to the performance room to hear what happened. Mr. Clift was honest, saying he didn't know much beyond the fact that the kids were really sick. He told Uncle Joe that the doctor would not tell him anything and that he was in the bus when it all happened. He blamed himself for being absent. Uncle Joe did not allow Mr. Clift to continue with that line of thought, telling him he had no way of knowing.

Uncle Joe needed to see the children and speak to their parents. He knew that even though he was not the trustee, in the eyes of the community, the buck stopped with him. He needed information quickly in order to respond to the inquiries that would surely come his way. Uncle Joe was uncomfortable because he had absolutely no knowledge of what happened, and within the hour, he needed to know everything. Where was Delong? Uncle Joe needed answers right away.

He decided it would be best for Mr. Clift to immediately excuse himself so he could clean up. Uncle Joe then left to visit the families of the sick children. After school, Mr. Clift returned to drive the remaining students home.

Uncle Joe drove first to the home of Midwife Annie Mae James hoping she would accompany him to the homes and assist him, but she was a step ahead, already out tending to the needs of the families. Eventually, he caught up with her, as she was administering time-tested home remedies to relieve burning, upset stomach and diarrhea. While her training was limited, her procedures were sufficient enough to treat most minor ailments. After a few days, it became evident that her treatments were not enough.

At the time, a popular herbal remedy was the feverfew leaf, a plant used to reduce nausea and vomiting. Another plant, called sweet clover, acted as a mild antiseptic. It was often used to heal burns and other types of wounds. The leaf of the wild strawberry was also used, infused as a tea, for aiding recovery from diarrhea.

Annie Mae had never seen these types of burns, as they were produced by a machine, but she was hearing one common theme: each child's parents wished they had never agreed to send their children for this so-called new treatment. Though greatly outmatched, Annie did her best to stabilize the children while providing what limited help she could.

When the parents saw Uncle Joe, they demanded answers about the treatments and reacted firmly when he appeared to have no knowledge. During the uproar, parents made it clear that permission was based on very little information and persuaded by fear. The parents wanted accountability, and Uncle Joe knew he would be first in line for that distinction.

As an administrator, Uncle Joe had never been so angry. He faced a pressure-sensitive situation. Among school principals, he was low on the power scale and he knew he could be easily replaced. Delong had kept Uncle Joe in the dark. It seemed that Uncle Joe was no better informed than the Lyles parents about the decisions made regarding the students. Even in his authoritative position, he was humiliated among those in his community.

It was not long before the Lyles community developed suspicions and fears of experimentation, though they had no idea of what kind. The parents knew nothing about the X-ray or radiation equipment held by the hospital. The parents agreed the problem was confined to Lyles Station.

Delong did not get his wish to remain anonymous. Pressure from unyielding parents did not subside. By now the children were experiencing frequent nightmares. Some children took much longer to recover than others, though eventually all were well enough to return to school. Parents rode the bus with their children, and many remained with them during the entire school day. At day's end, parents and students, together, boarded the bus for the ride home. In some cases this went on for weeks, as parents were dedicated to dispelling fears harbored by their children.

As weeks passed, parents received no answers. No one was angrier than Vertus' parents, Claude and Irene, who seethed at the thought of their sons unprotected when they handed them over to Delong.

The families were desperate for answers. They met at the hospital and insisted to see anyone who would meet with them. They were accused of trespassing and asked to leave. They refused. The hospital called the local police department who finally ordered the parents to vacate the premise or face arrest. Community elders told me that the families were not only orderly, but also prudent, in visiting the hospital, hopeful for answers. Without any help from the school trustee or Dr. Ellis, the parents were very much alone.

The harmful effects became more and more apparent as time passed. The affected children lost their hair in direct proportion to the amount of radiation they received. In the case of Vertus, his exposure was the worst, leaving him with more severe radiation burns and infectious lesions. The symptoms he faced, such as vomiting, headaches and dizziness, continued for weeks beyond the time frames of the other children. In fact, Vertus grew no hair for the remainder of his life.

During the same timeframe as these experiments, the photo below was taken of a young boy also treated by the hospital. The cause of his ailment is unknown, but the young boy seems to be feeling much better as a result of his treatment. By comparison, his parents must have found their experience with the hospital more pleasing. The photo captures a moment in time, a permanent record. The families of Lyles Station experienced the same hospital in a very different way. The only difference between the children was race.

Photo donated by Bruce Byers, Princeton Indiana. (Photo circa 1927)

Marguerite Russell Johnson, born 1919, was age ten at the time of the experiments. She was a student in Uncle Joe's class and shared about the sadness that remained when the children boarded the bus bound for the hospital. During an interview, Marguerite said, "I don't remember much these days, but one thing certain, I clearly remember that awful day." (Photo 2009)

"I don't understand why as children they did not see us as special, somehow not deserving what we got."

-Vertus

No Desire to Go

We held our discussions over breakfast. Uncle Gletus prepared a huge meal. The men remembered stories of feasting together when they were younger. Once we were finished, we reconvened in his living room and continued talking.

Returning to the story at hand, the men shared that their parents tried to cope as best they could with the uncertainty of what was done to their children. Within weeks of the experiment, Vertus' head resembled raw, torn flesh. His wound seldom dried long enough to produce a scab, severely hampering the healing process. The radiation choked off local blood vessels that transported oxygen rich blood needed for healing. The condition would appear to get better then suddenly take a turn for the worst.

Everything about his condition was compounded by his inability to grow hair. Parents, teachers, schoolmates and church members became primary protectors, shielding him from stares, teasing and ridicule. For months Irene worked on Vertus, sanitizing, dressing and generally overseeing his recovery. Nightmares continued as Vertus grew uncomfortable with the simplest electrical appliances. Vertus was awakened during the night by intense burning and nightmares recalling the words spoken by the technician, "Oh my God, I've given him too much." But his mother was always there to comfort him and help him through the night.

Parents' best efforts to learn what Dr. Ellis did to the children were met with silence; no one was talking. Uncle Joe was also kept in the dark, never learning the truth. Parents realized Uncle Joe had no knowledge of the scheme and removed any blame that would hinder an ongoing trusting relationship.

Within months, the time came for Vertus to enroll in school. He feared school tremendously, hoping with every ounce of his existence to avoid it. For him, school represented evil. Vertus told me, "I regressed to bed-wetting and had horrible nightmares. I associated the experiment with school." He went on to say, "I never wanted to have my sixth birthday because it also meant going to school."

When the day came, his mother escorted him and Melvin to the bus. Vertus continued, "My mother was so compassionate, she followed her heart. Thank God she did not force me to get back onto that bus until I was mentally ready. When the bus door swung open, and only Melvin boarded, my mama understood."

For the days that followed, Irene did things a little differently. This time she not only led Vertus and Melvin to the bus; she boarded with them. She made a promise not to leave Vertus' side for as long as he needed her. From that time, Irene rode the bus with her sons and spent the entire day in their classroom before again boarding the bus for home. This went on for weeks before Vertus developed the capacity to trust that Mr. Clift would never again take him back to the hospital.

Classmates, who never teased or made fun of them, respected all ten victims. A couple of the children who received lesser amounts of radiation grew a very thin layer of hair. However, in a matter of years, all the children lost their hair permanently. Vertus and Melvin received the greatest exposure to radiation as the last two children experimented on. Melvin faired far better than Vertus, having received less radiation. His recovery was much simpler.

During the school photo taken in 1928, which included the entire elementary grades one through three, Vertus and Melvin are pictured completely bald. Other completely bald children did not pose for this photo. As time passed, parents realized their condition was permanent and encouraged their children to participate in all photos. They placed hats on their children whenever they traveled outside of Lyles.

Lyles Station Consolidated School during school year 1928. Note that brothers Vertus and Melvin are bald. Vertus, third row just left of center; Melvin fourth row, right of center. When viewing the photo one can easily note the folded arms of the disciplinarian Uncle Joe standing back row center. Despite the era and its circumstances, Uncle Joe insisted that the children believe they were special beings capable of achieving their dreams.

Closer view shows Vertus (second from the left) with no hair. The girl wearing the hat behind him is Ella Mae Hardiman the only girl treated. She wears a hat to hide radical baldness and radiation burns. (Photo 1928)

Vertus was not pictured in the above photo because he was only five years old and not yet school age. First row, far right, sits Vertus' cousin Melvin (Fuzz) Hardiman, brother Melvin Hardiman on the third row, far left. Next to Melvin is cousin Horace Hardiman. By the next school photo, all the victims were completely bald. (Photo 1927)

HEARD FOR THE FIRST TIME

As our conversation progressed, the men remembered a significant meeting with a woman who would become important to their story. Her name was G'Anne Elliott. They erupted with stories about this caring woman, who was able to step into the situation and gain the trust of the Lyles Station community. She first met the Hardimans while shopping at the General Store.

Although the children wore caps, it was difficult to hide their unique condition. During a routine visit to town, the elderly woman approached the Hardimans. She had heard that children were recently treated with radiation and likely assumed the two boys, Melvin and Vertus were among those treated. She asked the question outright if their children were one of those treated with radiation. While the Hardiman parents were, as a rule, not interested in nosey spectators, their curiosity was piqued at the mention of radiation. Claude spoke up, "Yes, our boys were there."

Claude continued to unfold the story of how his boys came home with these burns after a treatment for ringworms. He introduced himself and his family. He was vulnerable, sharing his frustration with the incident and the resulting lack of information. He went on to explain to her the symptoms—the wounding and lack of hair regrowth. The Hardiman parents displayed their fear and concern before Mrs. Elliott.

Vertus said, "Mrs. Elliott took off our caps and looked at our heads." Melvin imagined she felt strongly that their family deserved answers. Vertus continued, "Our parents truly believed that she cared nothing about the fact that we were Negroes...she was a wonderful woman," he added. Though Vertus was younger, he also recalled her kindness.

"My parents always told me that she wore a smile similar to that worn by a Sunday school teacher," he said. Within days of their first meeting, she contacted the Hardimans.

Mrs. G'Anne Elliott was one of the most compassionate, energetic women in the community. She was an early riser and hard worker; it was rumored that she watered the garden, canned a batch of peaches then prepared a hearty full course meal before the average person rolled out of bed. (Photo circa 1948)

Vertus age five, Melvin seven with sister Vera age two. The Hardiman boys wore flat caps to shield themselves from ridicule. Mrs. Elliott recognized their condition despite the intended disguise. (Photo circa 1927)

"Our parents truly believed that Mrs. Elliott cared nothing about the fact that we were Negroes...she was a wonderful woman."

-Vertus

A Golden Spirit

It's been said that before you can give, you must have. In the case of Mrs. Elliott, she was blessed with material resources, but also had great compassion for those less fortunate. For decades, she had witnessed numerable injustices. By some fate, this case seemed to be a call to action for Mrs. Elliott. She felt the Hardimans' pain and eagerly sought to help them. The men shared a story about her certain determination.

Mrs. Elliott had no real experience as a "Rights" advocate and had lived all her life on the upside of town. She knew very little about Lyles Station, never having cause to visit. The Lyles Station parents didn't see her as one of those who told racist jokes or made light of the misfortune of others. On the contrary, the Elliotts were especially angered by the mistreatment of Negroes.

As it was in the 1920s, interaction across racial lines would not happen without controversy. Organizations, such as the Klan (KKK), instilled fear through violence toward any white person lending a hand to Negroes. The Elliotts understood this, and in the beginning, kept any activity behind closed doors. The experiments had spread through the broader community, generally a topic of conversation in social clubs, among women married to men of society. Mrs. Elliott had heard the rumors and the jokes about children receiving "eye-popping" levels of radiation. She was appalled and saw no humor in these depictions.

The Elliotts had a son named Jerrod, who was raised in his mother's shadow. He was born into this family of known sympathizers and was not surprised by his mother's concern for the Hardimans. The Elliott family had a long history of defending the rights of Negroes.

Mrs. Elliott's father fought in the Civil War as a member of the Union Army, and gave his life for that cause.

Jerrod Elliott had recently graduated from law school, and was in the process of preparing for the state bar exam. He was employed as a law clerk under the supervision of a full time lawyer and was not allowed to give legal advice. Furthermore, the firm he worked for specialized in securities and wills, and not with school children, hospitals, X-ray equipment or ringworm. He hoped to one day become a successful litigator in his own right, and he knew a case such as the one his mother was becoming involved in would not be a crowning insert onto his resume, a case where he would assist Negro plaintiffs against white leaders accused of wrong doing.

Jerrod and his mother agreed to meet with Claude and Irene. They spent the next few days preparing, reading article after article about radiation in anticipation of questions. They met with Mr. Clift, who gave his account freely, confirming the probability that the hospital intended to hide something. The Elliotts hoped to articulate some much desired facts about the experiments to Vertus' parents and hoped to deliver their message with as much compassion as possible.

When the meeting was finally underway, Mrs. Elliott began by telling Jerrod how she first met the Hardimans. She told him how she had noticed the children's baldness and was moved by the kindness and concern the Hardimans showed for their children.

The Hardimans were struck by her words and felt hopeful, they could trust her. They had no other real options and wisely chose to lay aside their pride. Claude told Mrs. Elliott, "We just want to know what they did to our children." Jerrod at this point joined the discussion, "What do y'all know about radiation?" At this question, Irene and Claude glanced at each other then back at Jerrod.

Jerrod went on to describe its poisonous properties, side effects and ability to cause real harm. He made it very plain, careful not to speak in technical terms. He pointed out what he alleged to be the hospital's purpose and what they stood to gain, information he acquired from hospital insiders. Jerrod told of the newly purchased equipment and the hospitals need to find subjects for testing purposes. "As he revealed the facts, it really got to my parents," Melvin said.

Vertus recalled his mom shouting, "Lord have mercy!" Jerrod dropped an even larger bomb when he used the word 'experiment,' unveiling the hospital's intent to treat the children as though animals. "When Jerrod said that, my dad hit the ceiling. He slammed his fist on the table and then excused himself for some fresh air," said Melvin.

Irene later told the story; how she closed her eyes and shuttered in reaction to Claude's anger. She said, "I had tears in my eyes and uttered her words quietly: Claude, we shouldn't have let those boys go." The Elliotts, seized by the moment of reaction, waited for the Hardimans. Mrs. Elliott responded to Irene's tears with tears of her own. Claude asked, "Where does all this leave the children, all ten of them?" Claude was likely thinking about the death and destruction from the radiation poisoning described by Jerrod. The enlightenment that came with the information finally afforded them, arrived with demoralizing pain.

Next, the Elliotts were introduced to the remaining parents. Claude and Irene wanted trust around the table and for others to accept the Elliotts as they had. The meeting convened at the home of Henry and Ora Mae Hardiman. It began with a general discussion of the status of the children and how they were coping. Some needed continual assistance to overcome apparent fears.

They shared the frustration of the constant questions that arose from their children, "Mama, what did I do to them?" Or, "Why did they do this to me?" The parents stated that their children were no longer the same, now uncertain in their actions. They wanted them to return to happier times when soap bubbles were magic and they believed their parents could protect them from anything.

Vertus remembered his mother shedding tears. He said, "Mama bribed me with offers of candy and cookies in exchange for me tolerating the pain when she changed my bandages." Vertus continued, "Those moments were reminiscent to her of earlier times, when she was a child. She asked her parents why so many outside her race treated her differently. For her, I think life had come full circle."

Mrs. Elliott spoke for the first time. She sensed the parents blamed themselves and she did not agree that they did anything wrong. She stunned the parents when she started by sharing her personal story, a lonely child moving from orphanage to orphanage in search of a special place to call home. She was not adopted until age sixteen. Gletus said, "At this point in the conversation, you could hear a pin drop." But, the parents still were not completely sure that they could trust her.

After breaking the ice, Mrs. Elliott moved the conversation along, seeking to get the parents talking so that she and Jerrod could sort out some facts. She asked questions and directed each of them to share their perspective of the incident. After about an hour of discussion they came to the conclusion that they needed help. They needed a lawyer, a white lawyer!

It would not be easy to find one, but Mrs. Elliott was determined to try. An old classmate named Winston Philpot was her first choice. Philpot made a career of cases involving city matters and the occasional criminal case. But none involved representing a Negro plaintiff against a white defendant. Philpot had children of his own and Mrs. Elliott felt he might sympathize with the families and at least, consider the case. She knew that convincing him was no small order.

When they met, Philpot eventually refused the case and encouraged the Elliotts to do themselves a favor and forget the idea. Mrs. Elliott informed Irene and Claude of the setback. The Hardimans were not surprised and understood the need for another strategy. They thought the odds were impossible to find a white lawyer, but Mrs. Elliott disagreed and was not ready to give up.

At Lyles Station, Uncle Joe and his wife visited Irene and Claude. Claude shared news about the rejection by the lawyer in spite of the sincere intentions of Mrs. Elliott. Uncle Joe suggested a Negro lawyer but Claude reminded him what Mrs. Elliott expressed, that a Negro lawyer could be easily marginalized. Uncle Joe then remembered a white lawyer from nearby Mount Carmel, the community bordering Lyles Station on the west. Elmer McGee once represented a Negro against his white accusers. This was very rare.

They took the information to the Elliotts. The Hardimans knew that the kind of skill and courage needed required someone willing to sacrifice popularity to fight for their rights. Mrs. Elliott contacted McGee for an appointment and this time, she brought Irene and her children. Uncle Joe also made arrangements to free up Mr. Clift's duties so he could join them.

Fortunately, Attorney McGee was much different from Philpot. He was an intense listener with incredible patience. He seemingly had nothing to prove to anyone. His gut and his conscience ruled. Mrs. Elliott described the victims and their parents along with perceived motives of the hospital. She mentioned the ringworm and the cloak of secrecy adopted by those involved. She added that there has been no medical care offered. Jerrod disclosed information from contacts at the hospital, including that of the new equipment and his research describing the danger from over exposure. The Elliotts told McGee how the children were part of a money making radiation experiment.

Irene described the scenario as recounted by Mr. Clift and shared Vertus' disfigurement and hair loss. Irene sat Vertus on her lap and removed his cap so McGee saw what she was describing. She stated, "I know who I placed on that bus that day, but now I have no idea what my child could become or the problems he could suffer tomorrow." It may have been that the sight of Vertus' scalp impacted him.

McGee shifted the tone and began asking questions about the home visits made by the school trustee. He recognized this as abnormal behavior and obvious intimidation. He also recognized the importance of the permission slips that fell short of providing details about the procedures to be performed. McGee communicated that these documents were key.

Vertus told stories told to him by his father. His father recounted that McGee conveyed to the Elliotts, "These kinds of experiments have gone on for decades; the mentally ill, prisoners, Negroes, etc." The Elliotts expressed ignorance as Attorney McGee asked, "Why does this surprise you?" McGee then stated, "Maybe this scene has played itself countless times, disguised as a method to kill some disease or other. Ringworm is as good an excuse as any, a fungus that spreads real fast, which translates into a larger selection pool. Then all of a sudden, you've got more than enough specimens for 'treatment' and no one is the wiser!"

McGee had a hunch that the hospital and school system had every reason to cover their tracks. He told Mrs. Elliott, "I see why you are involved with this. It won't be easy. I guess you want me to take the case." Irene's entire demeanor begged for his compassion. Mrs. Elliott responded, "And, Mr. McGee, gratis, without charging one cent that they don't have nor should have to raise." Irene later remembered this moment with clarity. "That woman was unbelievable," she said.

Perhaps Mrs. Elliott was bluffing, taking a risk that paid off. She added, "Well, maybe you can charge one dollar, that I will be responsible to pay. Heaven forbid a buzz surfacing that Fred McGee works for free." With a smile, McGee responded sarcastically, "Damn you…I'll charge you two!" It was Irene who let out the grateful response, "Thank you, thank you, thank you, Mr. McGee." Vertus knew this story, and knew it well.

"Our parents wanted us to return to happier times when soap bubbles were magic and we believed they could protect us from anything."

-Vertus

A Quarterback in Place

After the meeting with Attorney McGee, the Elliotts dropped Irene and the children at their home. Claude had worked that day, farming the fields since dawn. Irene, noticing he was not in the house, headed directly to the bell. She rang him in by using a mealtime cadence. Recently there had been little to smile about; but today that changed. They had a lawyer. Claude expected, at best, a report of the lawyer's consideration of their request. But the truth was more than Claude could imagine. Irene added, "The Elliotts were the good luck charm we needed."

Weeks later, the first meeting with their newly retained counsel was called. The parents now had a number of areas covered: an investigator, researcher, informant and McGee himself, all ready to work on behalf of the children. Together Negroes and Whites worked on the case—unheard of during that time.

No one was following the ordeal any closer than Wayman Chapel Church in Lyles Station. Since the earliest of times, the church was the focal point for information. The team attended a service held in their honor. On Sunday, the church was filled to capacity. Following service, church members reconvened in the fellowship hall to a feast designed to express appreciation for the team's time and contributions. The pastor prayed, asking that no other child ever again suffer similarly.

Vertus shared that his mother later told him how they couldn't believe the amount of love and forgiveness being spoken of by the parishioners. Mrs. Elliot told Irene that she was amazed that she never heard the words revenge or anger mentioned in the course of the entire service.

Before the banquet was over, Mrs. Elliott went to Irene and asked if she would take Vertus to meet attorney McGee. He squatted down to Vertus as Mrs. Elliott removed his cap. McGee saw the same innocence that Mrs. Elliott spoke of, the innocence that led her to commit to this cause. The absence of hair, or even color on Vertus' scalp was powerfully persuasive. His burned ears, forehead and unsightly lesions were noticeable. This and the generous attitude of the community sealed the team's commitment to this case and its mission.

The parents learned that McGee was a graduate of the University of Indiana law school. His first order of business was a visit to his college professor and mentor. McGee wanted help to decide the best approach to winning this case. There were things he needed to familiarize himself with, such as school procedures and protocols, field trip authorization and radiation. He would look deeper into the economic history of the hospital to prove motive for their actions.

His charge was that the hospital recruited the students for the experiment, with no intention of curing ringworm. Perhaps his greatest challenge was to obtain a judgment of win for the rights of all children versus a loss for ten Negro children.

McGee really didn't know what to expect. The only other time he represented a Negro was a client accused of theft. McGee offered a plea of not guilty. A powerful and vengeful prosecutor sought to convict an innocent man. McGee was masterful, winning an acquittal. Now, on the offense, his case would have to be even stronger.

McGee worked very hard developing the case. Eventually, he filed a complaint on behalf of the children of Lyles Station in the Princeton courthouse. Vertus recalled the facts of the case stating, "When I was in high school I found a copy of the complaint. One of my teachers had it. She was curious why our heads looked so strange."

McGee alleged the children were willfully and maliciously experimented on resulting in massive abuse, disfigurement and physical calamity yet unknown. He also alleged a conspiracy to violate the rights of the students. Named defendants included the county hospital, the school system, Mr. Delong, Dr. Ellis and the makers of the radiation equipment.

Several whites also expressed concern for the children and fully aligned with McGee. They approved of his taking the case and felt those responsible should be punished. He received letters of encouragement as well as hate mail. Ignoring it all, McGee hoped for a swift trial to avert witness intimidation, because if the trial lingered, community pressure would intensify and so would the threats.

After adhering to proper procedures and filing protocol, they received a date and the hearing began. McGee laid out his evidence to prove the treatments were experiments constituting a severe violation of the children's rights. Plainly put, he alleged that the parents were tricked. McGee had the parents testify that Delong told them of a new treatment that was heretofore available only to white children, and as a result of his lobbying efforts, this procedure had become available to Negro children. They were led to believe that Delong cared. "It was a real good feeling," declared one parent.

The tone in the courtroom was intense. The judge barred the children from the proceeding, ordering them to attend school. The court never witnessed their injuries or heard their firsthand accounts. The defense argued that detailed descriptions of the procedure were given and that parents gave their permission for all that occurred. Even though the equipment was newly acquired, the hospital described the treatment as a standard medical practice and not an experiment. The hospital described itself as an upstanding institution that would never inflict harm on anyone.

The subject of negligence was not addressed by the defense, albeit the technicians did not appear qualified to operate the equipment. Subsequently, the accused were acquitted.

The men of Lyles Station recalled these facts, told to them by their parents who sat through the proceedings. They stated that there was never an official recognition of the tragedy, nor any remorse ever expressed on the part of the accused. Parents took the verdict as a setback even though they knew at the inception that legal action against the perpetrators would not be easy. The hardest thing to accept was watching their children suffer.

Parents were left to carry the guilt alone, some for the remainder of their lives. Irene, while on her deathbed in 1999 (72 years later), just before passing, hugged her sons for the last time. While doing so she gave a final apology for her decision to place them on that bus in 1927. "Vertus and Melvin," she whispered, "I'm sorry. Mother didn't mean any harm, I just didn't know." They both acknowledge today that before their mother died, they assured her she was forgiven and asked her to let go of her burden. At that point, through teary eyes, Melvin and Vertus demonstrated just how much they adored their mother.

For the victims, life returned to normalcy, resuming as it did before the experiment. There was the occasional bully from outside of Lyles that pulled their caps and tossed them during a cruel game of keep-away. But for the most part, those in Lyles saw these children for what they were, real living souls with names and emotions, and they were treated as such.

As for Dr. Ellis, each evening the boys saw him driving down the main highway in route to his home. Vertus said, "As he drove by, we told each other, there goes that doctor that did this to us!" And for Delong, he completed one additional term as school trustee and was not reappointed.

Mrs. Elliott and the parents remained friends; in fact Mrs. Elliott called on each of them occasionally and in return encouraged them to visit her. She and Irene remained especially close until Mrs. Elliott's death in 1952. Lyles Station was well represented at her services. During the program, Claude and Irene went to the microphone together, encouraged by the Elliott family, to share a word in her memory. The Hardimans named her before others, a dear friend with a golden spirit.

After this discussion, I felt great about the data I had gathered. Now, I wanted to travel the city and visit some historical sites. I thanked the men again for their time, though they offered overwhelming gratitude to me. I stopped taping and agreed to see them again before our departure.

One Friday night at the Karaoke Lounge, I heard a song entitled *Don't Play That Song.* The lyrics ask that a song not be played because it brings back bad memories. It speaks about forgetting something from the past, ironic in its own telling. I thought of the trial those in Lyles Station had tried so hard to forget.

"I have my health and strength, can see and hear and I'm in my right mind. Those are blessings...three blessings."

-Vertus

They Knew Him When

On this day, Vertus and I took to the city. As we traveled, I was allowed to see Vertus in a new way. I watched old time neighbors and friends show love and respect for him in a way similar to the response of friends in California. I saw people, both black and white, approach him and proudly introduce themselves as family.

A white man greeted us on his front lawn and explained to Vertus that he was his nephew, a relation born of an interracial marriage. Vertus responded with a smile and warm embrace that made this colorblind scene so beautiful. The family members seemed proud to share kin with someone of a different race. Scenes like this, coupled with rural-town hospitality, made a very special day and I realized just how much of life was meant to be like this—members of the human race coming together.

For all the light moments, there were sad memories too. I was particularly moved when Vertus spoke about the teasing and described his need to hide from the truth of who he is. While driving, Vertus stated, "Imagine living your life in fear of being seen. My head is so ugly…I wish it wasn't. And as if that weren't enough, people never just accepted that and let me be. They were secretly cruel, always looking for ways to use my flaws against me. They wanted to see my ugliness then use it to hurt me. They screamed at the sight of me and turned away."

I filmed his statement and when Vertus finished speaking these words, it was more than I could handle. I turned away from him and began walking in the direction of the car saying, "I'll be right back, my battery is low." But my battery was fine. The truth was, I didn't want him to know that I was crying. I knew Vertus loved me but at the same time, I knew it was persons like me, along with others that he spoke about. I came to really understand Vertus and appreciated learning about his daily trials.

We then visited his ninety-nine year old aunt, Helen Hardiman. She reminisced about the experiments; she was a seventeen-year-old junior at Lincoln High. She stated, "The community's mood was very sad and regretful." She particularly remembered Ella Mae Hardiman describing how her hair fell out in thickets and the burns and scars left in its place. She told about the silent treatment given the parents by the school trustee and hospital. Helen stated, "It was years before Lyles Station folks would again trust the hospital. The anger and distrust cut real deep."

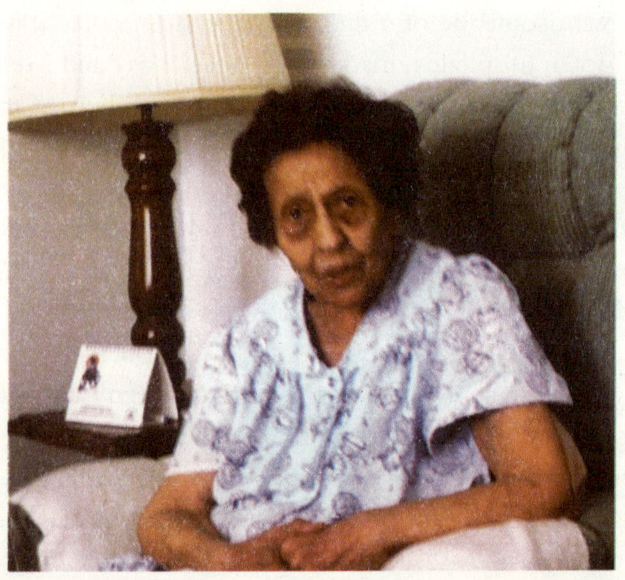

Aunt Helen Hardiman age ninety-nine. (Photo 2007)

After a short while we left Helen and traveled to the home of Edna Pearl Frye. At the time, Edna was soon to reach one hundred years and had lived in Lyles Station all her life. Her memory was still sharp as she told stories about school days in the old log cabin school and matriculating to Lincoln High School. For many years she was the pianist for Wayman Chapel Church.

Ms. Frye remembered the experiments. She knew the students since birth and vividly recalled their ordeal. She told of their tragic condition and the intrigue surrounding what actually happened. She also drew attention to Mrs. Elliott. She said, "I remember Mrs. Elliott. She helped us so and was so disappointed about the whole thing." Ms. Frye added details about the church praying for the children's strength and wellness. I changed the subject and asked, "What is the secret of living so long?" She responded, "Maybe it's the Lyles Station air."

After we left Ms. Frye's, we decided to take a ride and capture images of countryside. We rode along the old dirt roads and looked across acres of farmland. Vertus stared out the window as if searching for someone. He pointed out things such as a place where a family member worked or a farm that once belonged to someone he knew. Once in particular, he said, "Wilbert, look at the sun setting over the horizon. Isn't that lovely? There is nothing else like it."

Vertus was right. I couldn't help but appreciate the orange and gold prism that sprayed across the evening sky. Vertus continued telling me, "I remember these beautiful sunsets. My entire family would sit on the porch during the summers and enjoy them."

It was time to end our wondrous day. I was considerate of Vertus, careful not to challenge his stamina. We also kept track of time because Vertus' wound needed refreshing, so we returned to the hotel.

Edna Frye, soon to be 100 years of age. A gentle sweet lady who has a way of making you feel quite at home. Mr. Clift, the driver who in 1927 transported the children, was her father's first cousin.

Back at the hotel, Vertus immediately started the process of re-dressing his wound. He told me that he spent about ninety dollars per month on medical supplies, for things like gauze, gloves, ointments and the like. He took antibiotics regularly to eliminate unpleasant odors. Also key to his maintenance was a twice daily flushing of the wound with saline water. The pressure from the spray was strong enough to dislodge unwanted residue. Following the wash, an application of prescription crème was applied before laying sterile gauze across.

Vertus then meticulously tied a night cover around his head or in the case of his morning wash, covered the wound with his beanie. In either case, the process required one hour and nineteen minutes. This procedure occurred twice every day.

A look at Vertus just prior to bedtime, the wound had been washed and medications were applied. (Photo 2007)

"There are times when I underestimated the value of family until they were gone."

-Vertus

An Empty Bed

It was three in the morning when I looked at Vertus' bed to find it empty. I assumed he was somewhere in the room possibly in the bathroom. I didn't think much of it and rolled over to return to sleep. I expected to hear him return to the room at any moment. Time went by and I heard nothing. I thought maybe he left, out visiting a friend or relative? After all, we were in his hometown, and someone could have come by and got him, right?

But then I began to think about it. Would Vertus leave without a word? I tried not to worry, believing he'd come through the door any second, with a snack or toting a bucket of ice to sooth his scalp. After about an hour, I felt compelled to look for him. I dressed then walked towards the entry door. I stopped suddenly, to my right was Vertus, lying asleep on the floor inside the small space situated between the entry door and the bathroom.

Picture in your mind the traditional floor plan found in most average priced hotels. There is a small room just large enough to house a vanity on one wall and a small closet equal in dimension on the opposite wall. It was on the floor in that small area that Vertus slept. He had removed the top sheet and blankets from his bed and transferred them onto the floor. It was a heart-tugging moment for me to see him struggle with something I took for granted. If the table were turned, I would find the floor incredibly uncomfortable. I was witnessing the high cost Vertus paid daily to manage such a simple activity as sleep.

Later that morning, I asked him about his sleeping habits and what led him to leave his bed. He said he was hurting—"My head was on fire. It happens often and it wakes me up." Vertus explained that the pain is intensified by anything that touches his scalp. I asked about the last time he remembered a peaceful night without interruption, Vertus could not tell me. And when he did sleep, he was so often interrupted by nightmares, especially the voice of that technician saying, "Oh my God, I gave him too much."

We left the hotel about 9 am and met with the chairman of the Lyles Station Historic Preservation Corporation. He gave us a tour of the newly renovated consolidated school. The building was stripped to its foundation then reconstructed to resemble its original architecture. Private and public grants made the project possible. Once the construction was completed, alumni of the school gave memorabilia, furniture, books and historical photos. Most of the furnishings are over one hundred years old.

I listened as Vertus relived his days as a student. He described the games he played, the spelling bees and musical performances. And this comment, "I was so shy around girls, I never had the courage to interact with them." We entered the classrooms Vertus attended while assigned to grades 1-3, 4-5 and grades 6-8. Vertus even recalled his seat assignment and went directly to it to sit. He spoke about his teachers and the impact they had on his life. My heart was recovering a little to see him so happy while recalling the good times he experienced in Lyles Station.

Stan Madison, chairman of the Lyles Station Consolidated School Foundation is an historian for the community. Here he provided a tour of the old schoolhouse and discusses with me historical times.

Before arriving, I prearranged a meeting with school alumni from the 1920s and 30s to recount the experiments of 1927. So, later on this day, we met with them to receive their input. Among the group were Alice Berry, Josephine Church, Gletus Hardiman, Imogene Stewart-Hughes, Flora Jackson, Alma Jones, Delbert Jones, Glenn Morris and Elsie Morse. Imogene Stewart-Hughes is the sister of Milburn Stewart (now deceased), one of the original ten victims. The group praised the school for their educational foundation. They praised school principal Joe Lucas, referring to him as the worthy captain of the ship.

They also remembered the ringworm fungus and the experiments. I was surprised at the detail of their stories and just how much the story has been told. They stated it was the luck of a draw in terms of which students became affected by the ringworm fungus and subsequently, a victim. Glenn stated, "I had the ringworm, but my parents said no thank you, we'll use the medication." Josie shivered as she asserted, "That could have been any one of us...me instead of Vertus." The thought made her cry.

They told of the humiliation the children experienced by curious onlookers because of their baldness and scarring. Imogene remembered the question her brother Milburn was most frequently asked, "What happened to you?" It seemed much easier for him to hide under a hat than to face the stigma surrounding human curiosity and stereotypes.

Alumni of Lyles Station had vivid memories of the ringworm outbreak, the experiments and the subsequent hardships on the students and their families. (Photo 2006)

We left the school very happy to have connected with its alumni. When we stepped outside, I was surprised to see flies hovering around Vertus' beanie. It was hours since we last cleansed his wound, which meant secretion was beginning to accumulate. The sight reminded me of what happened while aboard the plane from California.

Vertus fell asleep beneath the air conditioning vent that was opened to full capacity. The air bounced directly off his beanie causing a distinct odor to fill the cabin. People were complaining and asking questions about the smell. I immediately recognized the odor but never before recalled it being so distinct and strong. I suspected it was the air blowing above him pushing the odor around the cabin. I got up, went to him, and closed the overhead vent without his having any knowledge of the incident. In fact, he slept through the entire ordeal.

Today, the scene was similar. Apparently his wound wrappings were soiled and needed changing. Since we were outdoors however, flies circled around his head, like an episode from a children's cartoon. He had no way of knowing it was happening, that the flies were even there.

"I learned a long time ago that you can't get ahead when trying to get even."

-Vertus

FORGIVEN BUT NOT FORGOTTEN

We decided to return to the hotel and redress the wound before visiting Melvin "Fuzz", a resident of the local assisted living facility. It was twelve years since Vertus last saw him. "Personally, I would be remiss if I left Indiana without first visiting Fuzz, particularly given his serious condition," stated Vertus. Fuzz was age 86, suffering from a recent stroke. The stroke left him unable to provide for himself most of the measurable activities of daily living.

We arrived at the convalescent home and rang the doorbell. I cupped my hands against the glass to create a peephole. When I looked into the facility there was a hallway lined with rooms on each side. I also saw Fuzz seated in a wheelchair just a few feet inside the glass window. "Wow," I thought, amazed, I told Vertus and Horace that it was Fuzz without ever before seeing him. I recognized very familiar Hardiman features but most of all, I recognized the Hardiman features and the look of complete baldness even though Fuzz wore a baseball cap. When the door was electronically released we entered.

I was thrilled to meet the final surviving victim. I could see the pain still fresh in the hearts of Vertus and Horace grieving Fuzz's unfortunate state. We attempted interaction but Fuzz showed little response. I reached for the wheelchair brake release and began pushing him away from the door. I wanted to get him to his room, anxious to fully absorb the moment and pleasure of finally meeting him.

Immediately a nurse headed our way. Horace appeared to recognize her and began a dialogue. "This is Dr. Smith from California. He's writing a book on what happened to us when we were little boys. Dr.

Smith came to see my brother's head." My response was an internal "Oh no! Why did Horace say that?" The nurse's reaction was predictable. She stopped me in my tracks, removed the wheelchair from my grasp and proceeded to wheel Fuzz in a direct line to her supervisor.

The supervisor recited a privacy doctrine and stated that a California physician had no jurisdiction in Indiana. She added that the only person able to authorize my interaction with Fuzz was he himself or his sister Alberta. It was clear Fuzz was in no condition to give permission leaving only Alberta as sole grantor. Horace retrieved his cell phone and dialed her.

Horace then explained to Alberta the situation before handing his phone to the supervisor. Following the discussion the supervisor looked at me and said, "I'm gonna close the door to Mr. Hardiman's room for just 30 minutes...30 minutes is all you have." She escorted us to Fuzz's room, left the room and closed us in.

Fuzz suffered his stroke in 2006. Most times he would stare into space unaware of those around him. I washed my hands in preparation of removing his baseball cap and bandages. There were four circular shaped bandages protecting four lesions on his scalp. Horace began to share history of the wound and its advancement throughout time. I assumed like Vertus these lesions were hallowed areas of the skull. Perhaps Fuzz too would see his skull bone rip away.

I later learned the convalescent hospital had no knowledge of the excessive radiation exposure and subsequently explained away the lesions on Fuzz's head as common bedsores. Vertus and I advised them of the correct cause of the breakdown. We were explicit in our information, warning against the application of unnecessary pressure for fear of potential breaks in his skull. Of course they were alarmed, and very much surprised.

We concluded our private time with Fuzz. As promised, the supervisor returned as I reapplied fresh bandages. Once she saw the bandages reapplied, we opened the door and stayed a couple of hours before leaving. I was glad to have finally placed five victims into their story and noted their physical similarities. As I left Fuzz, I shook my head realizing the devastation endured by the entire Hardiman family. My heart went out to them and the Stewart family.

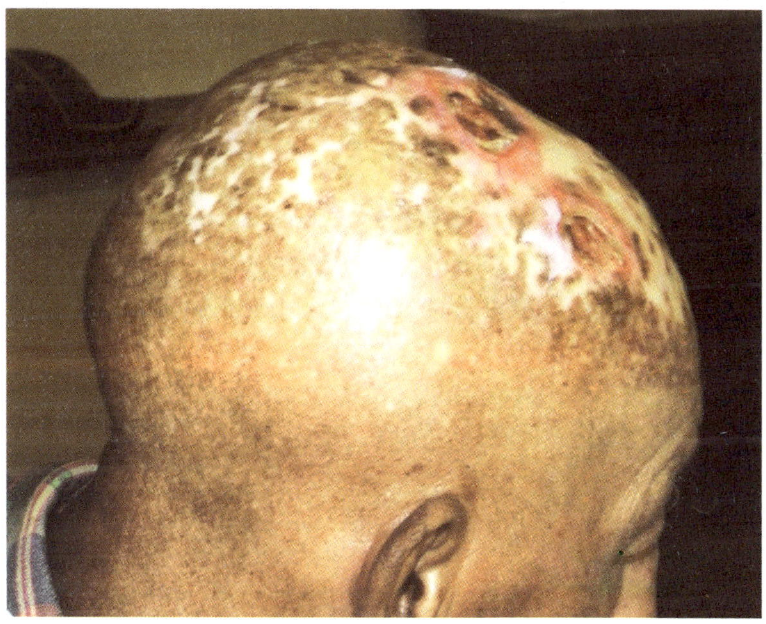

Above is a photo of Melvin "Fuzz" Hardiman. Note the crusting of the upper portions of his ears just like the others, the result of the large hat like device placed upon his head as a child. It is assumed that Fuzz did not receive as much radiation as Vertus. He is the young boy pictured in the lower right corner of the class photo taken in 1927.

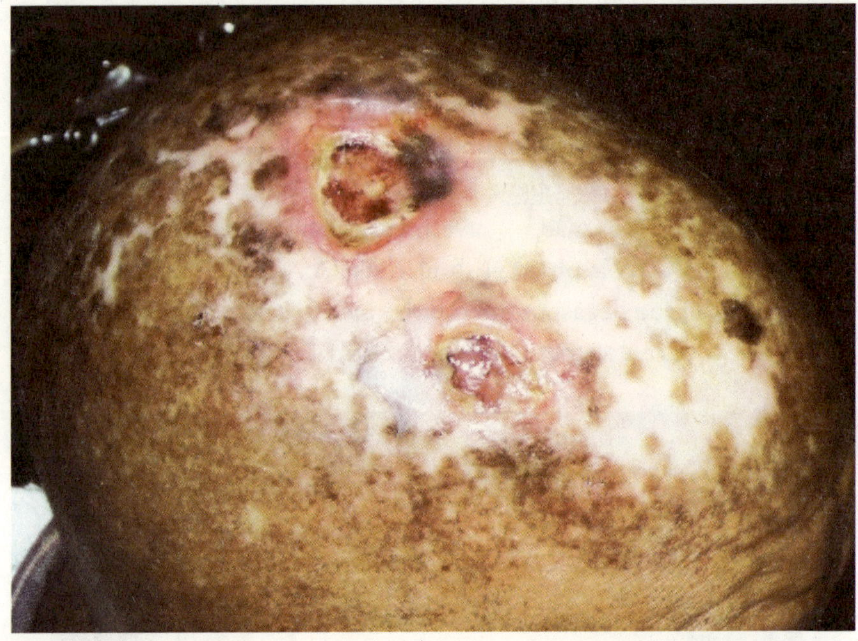

Fragile areas of Fuzz's skull…I suggested the family alert his caregivers of the potential danger of skull breakage if undue pressure were applied to the lesions.

Back To The Dungeon

Now, it was time for the biggest part of our trip, a visit to the hospital. I'd left this part for last, careful not to offend anyone so soon or make anyone feel unnecessarily uncomfortable. Horace, Gletus and Melvin had no interest in joining us, but Vertus was determined to accompany me. Today, Vertus would nervously face his demon for the first time in eighty years. We said goodbye to the men and headed to the hospital. We arrived at about 2 pm.

I was immediately struck by the building's old style architecture. I had a vision of the hospital as a dungeon like, sinister place. I imagined it a ghostly haunt from generations past, entombed by wooden boards nailed across doors and windows. Reason told me there was a good side to the hospital, represented by medical treatment and improved lives over many years. Understandably, Vertus saw things differently, and this affected my perception.

When I first saw the hospital, I recalled the stories of how some were never allowed to enter the front doors, and were instead forced to enter the halls through the rear. I mentioned to Vertus the pride I felt, knowing that society had remedied such discriminations. He agreed with me, but my statements did little to calm him, which was my intent.

As Vertus and I drew closer, I didn't stop directly in front of the hospital. I drove slowly and passed the location, circling the block a time or two. I thought this might also calm Vertus a bit. He was noticeably shaken, if not outright agitated. After my second trip around the hospital, he raised his voice and asked me, "Wilbert, why are you passing it by so much? Let's just stop. I'm ready!" Eventually, I parked directly across from the hospital's entrance. I grabbed my still camera and camcorder. I wanted to have my video camera rolling to capture these significant moments. I was without a script as I began to film.

I first asked Vertus to describe where we were, our reason for being here. He responded, "We're at the hospital where I was experimented on when I was five years old, where I was burned and scarred and lost all my hair." Incredibly, it dawned on me that I just heard the voice of the little boy inside Vertus, the child of five, voicing disappointment carried for eighty years. Possibly it was this little boy who was angriest at losing his hair. His voice reminded me of years filled with frustration, speaking without being heard. I briefly turned the camera off and we continued in silence.

Vertus pointed to the basement windows as the place where the experiments happened. I recall the eerie chill that blanketed me as he pointed. The building was old and in need of repair, however, given its age of more than 100 years, it wasn't that bad looking. It was situated in a residential neighborhood, single-family houses on all sides. Across the street were additional homes; one of them functioned as living quarters for the hospital's nursing staff during the 1920s.

In 1927, Mr. Clift drove onto the hospital grounds and parked the school bus in the rear. The lower level windows mostly covered by white panels represent the basement where the experiments took place.. (Photo 2006)

I stood on the opposite side of the street using a wide-angle shot to capture the full scope of the building. I was now ready for a closer look. We crossed the street and made ready for a closer view. I noticed a sign staked into the ground quite similar in style to that of a realtor's ad to sale. It was advertising an accounting business. I thought this was an outdated sign representing a prior occupant, assuming this building was abandoned. I continued operating my camcorder and to my astonishment, I saw a light glowing in one of the rooms. Can it be that someone was there? I was excited!

I thought to myself that if we could get in there under any circumstances, it would be a jackpot of major proportions and a rare opportunity to reenter that day in 1927. I said to Vertus, "Come on! Somebody's in there." Vertus seemed dazed, perhaps uncertain as to whether or not he wanted to enter a place he once promised never again to visit. Walking ahead, I led the way up a short flight of stairs with Vertus directly behind me. When we reached the landing, I turned off the power on my camcorder and placed it in my carrying case.

I wondered if Vertus was all right. He was so timid, and clearly hiding behind me as if I was his protector. I never before saw him this fragile, but I completely understood. It was 1927 again, perhaps the same fears as that morning 80 years ago. Vertus later said, "I was in the experiment all over again in my mind, screaming for a way to escape. I could hear the music and see the technicians."

This was the old nurse's quarters, directly across from the hospital. (Photo 2006)

I turned the handle on the old style doorbell that rang for as long as the visitor continued to twist its handle. There was no immediate response so I rang it again. Just before I released the second turn the huge door swung open. There a lady stood who issued the salutation, "Hello, how may I help you?" I swallowed hard. At that moment I felt like Sherlock Holmes there to solve a mystery. Vertus stood approximately two feet behind me. I couldn't see his demeanor, but I assumed my sidekick was holding up and playing his part.

Rita was her name. She was a middle-aged lady, dressed rather conservatively with mannerisms to match. I replied, "Hello, I'm Dr. Wilbert Smith, a writer from California. My friend is the subject of a biographical story, Mr. Vertus Hardiman. His story includes the old hospital. We wondered if it was possible that we come in for a few moments." Rita aimed her attention at Vertus in response to my introduction. She asked, "Well, you must be important." Vertus smiled a bit as she continued, "Come on in, I'll get the owner."

Wow! This would be really great, a firsthand look at the place where the experiments happened. I did not want this to backfire on me and force me to have Vertus carried out on a stretcher! I expected exterior photos but never in my wildest dreams did I anticipate actual entry. Rita invited us in, offered us seats then left to find the owner. I later learned the owner was her husband. When Rita left, I whispered to Vertus, "Hang in there, I've got this." I knew this was huge for him requiring incredible courage.

We were not at all dressed for the part. Vertus wore his wool beanie in the extremely hot, 102-degree temperature along with a blue jumpsuit similar to the style worn in the 1970s. And as for me, I was also dressed a bit too casual wearing blue jeans and a white tee shirt.

Vertus pictured just before our visit to Gibson general hospital. (Photo 2006)

A gentleman came in, shook our hand and introduced himself as Bruce Byers. On the surface he seemed upbeat and friendly which gave me optimism. He seemed proud to be the building's owner; particularly knowing the hospital was part of an old story. Bruce said, "Well I'm glad to know you. You've come a long way; you say you're from California?" I responded, "Yes, we both are." I immediately apologized for showing without an appointment and he told me it was fine because it was not his busiest time of the year.

Bruce told us, "I love learning stories associated with the hospital's history." He then seemed to look at Vertus for a comment. I was not sure he was ready to engage Bruce still attempting to adjust from the uneasiness brought on by the hospital's surroundings. I shielded Vertus by stalling through conversation, allowing him additional time to relax.

I asked Bruce if he received frequent visitors. He responded, "Not too many" and reminded me he was running a business. Also the old hospital was a common fixture to locals. Bruce said, "Even I was born in Gibson County and remembered walking past the hospital and smelling the distinct odor of ether." He also recalled many of the primitive procedures, but he knew little about the hospital of the 1920s.

I told Bruce about Vertus and the children from Lyles Station but wondered how I could comfortably mix in the story of the experiments. But for certain, I welcomed his compassion. I looked for a story or two seeking to establish a rapport with him. I shared the stories I learned, about two beds in the basement reserved for Negroes and the call button used to call down a nurse working on an upper floor. This information came thanks to aunt Alice from Lyles Station. Bruce told me, "I've seen the wires dangling from the basement ceiling but never knew their use."

I told Bruce, "As a writer, I find stories such as that fascinating. Would you repeat that historical account on camera?" Bruce answered, "I'll do my best." I turned on the camera and once we were done Bruce asked, "How was that?" I responded, "Oscar worthy." At this point I sensed his buy-in.

I asked Vertus to remove his beanie, revealing all but the actual wound covered by additional dressing. Bruce saw enough to appeal to his heart and responded to the request of a short tour with "I think we can do that." I followed him and Vertus while operating my camcorder. He began by introducing Vertus and me to his staff. They were seated in offices once used as patient rooms. Vertus seemed noticeably more comfortable thanks to Bruce, who was making him feel better. I welcomed this because I was truly concerned about his reaction.

Bruce's business occupied about half of the main floor. His clients were kept from viewing the floor's unoccupied portions by a large drape, designed to hide the unfurnished portion of the first floor. But it was the dreaded basement that I was most interested in viewing and it was possibly the least desired part of the tour for Vertus.

[illegible]ally, the moment arrived. Bruce reached into his pocket to get a [illegible]e oversized key to unlock a door that led to a stairway leading to the basement. At this point my mind was playing detective. I wondered why the basement had a unique key, as though this level was so distant from the rest of the building, as though we were reaching restricted areas. It led to the mystique of the old building, finally uncovered by Vertus 80 years later.

Bruce turned the key and proceeded to yank at the door in an attempt to open it. This occurred amidst a very loud scrubbing noise, the result of the oversized door dragging across the floor. The stairway was real spooky, dark and hardly traveled, as evidenced by the thick accumulation of spider webs draped across the stairway's opening. We cleared them with a broom before proceeding downward. There was no lighting, so we were forced to depend on Bruce's handheld flashlight and the light mounted atop my video camera. Bruce led the way and gave constant warnings to watch our step.

I asked Bruce, "How often do you visit the basement?" He responded, "Only when necessary…only when I have to. It's usually for maintenance related issues. In fact, it has been almost a year since I was last down here."

The basement was chilly and had a musty unoccupied smell. There were dead pigeon carcasses, rain gutters, antique file cabinets, an old telephone switchboard and plumbing parts scattered about. I kept my camera rolling amid what seemed to be an obstacle course.

I also attempted to keep in close proximity to Vertus constantly making sure he was okay. I caught a glimpse of his slow, calculated walk, stepping cautiously as though testing floorboards for loose or broken planks. For the moment, he was a young boy needing my watchful eye. He assured me that so far all was fine. I told him I would trust his judgment then returned to filming.

Bruce Byers leading Vertus and Wilbert into the dreaded basement of the old hospital. (Photo 2006)

Bruce pointed to an area that once housed a kitchen, dining area and boiler room. Finally he led us to the area that once housed a room designated for x-ray. It was in the x-ray area when Vertus took the lead, assuming the role as tour guide. His first few sentences were short and to the point. I could tell he was not completely comfortable. But his memory was so vivid, sharp and filled with incredible detail. Judging by Bruce's reactions, he seemed to welcome the added history Vertus provided. He proceeded to add a sentence here and there to color the story. Vertus stated, "I was crying and ever so nervous…I shook all over. I held on to my brother Melvin because I thought he would somehow protect me."

Vertus told us about the students, identifying where they stood and lined up. He stated, "We wanted to believe Mr. Clift when he said we would not be hurt. But in the end, we hurt all over." Vertus described the smell of burning hair and the sound of loud music playing during the experiment. He explained how the young boys wanted to appear strong for Ella Mae, the only female victim. He pointed out the location where they lined up and the approximate place he and Melvin were before the experiment. At this point he was swelling with emotion. His voice cracked as he described the three rooms involved in the experiment.

The basement of Gibson General hospital as viewed by Vertus. (Photo 2006)

By the time he mentioned his treatment he paused then completely stopped the story. I knew Vertus reached a critical point and maybe both of us were relieved, as we bravely stepped through this. After minutes, Vertus was again calm as though a mental promotion occurred. He no longer seemed nervous and his voice became normal. He borrowed Bruce's flashlight, and, on his own, explored small areas of the basement. It was apparent that closure was finally occurring. While Bruce and I stood there alone, Bruce mentioned, "Dr. Smith, this has truly been a pleasure. Vertus seems to be a very nice guy. Do you think this was helpful?" I responded, "More than you could ever imagine."

We returned up the stairs and, as though ceremoniously scripted, once we reached the landing, Bruce allowed Vertus to close the basement door, maybe hoping Vertus would never to see or open this door or ever open it again. Vertus thanked Bruce and his staff with the following words, "Well Bruce, we sure want to thank you for taking time to show us around. This has truly been a blessing!" I believe Vertus really meant these words.

I, too, thanked Bruce for the experience while turning off my camcorder. As we left the building, we walked down the walkway towards the street. Just before the sidewalk was a short handrail to assist in stepping downward. Once there, Vertus, standing just behind me, grabbed my shoulder and began a short prayer thanking the Lord for this day and all it had brought. During the prayer he began to cry.

In a peaceful moment of solitude, I heard him say words of thanks for strength to confront lifelong fears. He said, "Those demons have finally released me. Now I can replace them with a flock of doves here to guide me home." Amazing! Home, to me, has always meant heaven. Was Vertus saying that he is now better prepared to close his life here on earth?

Following the short prayer he seemed deep in thought. We got into the car and amongst deafening silence I drove towards the hotel. Vertus did not speak a word while staring at the highway. I knew what we just did was powerful and no doubt he was proud to have buried many fears, hopefully forever. Vertus did not say anything until we arrived at the hotel.

As I turned off the engine Vertus looked to me and said, "I sure miss Mr. Clift. He was a good man, a real good man." I replied, "I know, I remember him...he was the bus driver that day and also your uncle."

Vertus smiled then nodded in the affirmative, obviously pleased that I remembered!

At this moment, he was possibly releasing something extremely important, and I wasn't quite ready to move on. I asked about the female technician, whose character by now was described as the lone voice within his lifelong nightmares. I asked if it were possible that he also closed the basement door on her and her spoken words, "Oh my God, I've given him too much." Vertus was able to answer the question only by the words, "With God's help."

Later that night, Vertus offered a more complete reaction to visiting the hospital. I sensed he was genuine and honest in his response. He said, "I never thought I would ever see that place again. But I am glad I came back and got the chance to close that basement door." He added, "I am no longer held captive in that basement."

I was never able to completely comprehend what those words meant, but I do recall thinking the just completed experience was very therapeutic. I was glad I was a part of Vertus' newfound freedom. Vertus feel asleep shortly after this conversation. He later told me that he rested better that night than others in recent memory.

Vertus and Bruce are touring the basement while sharing painstaking details of the experiments. Bruce was a terrific guy who took an instant liking to Vertus.

The prayer following the hospital exit when Vertus thanked God for that day and all it had brought. He was grateful for the required strength to face his lifelong inner-dwelling demons. (Photo 2006)

THE RINGWORM CHILDREN

Our trip had come to an end. Before heading to the airport, we stopped by Melvin's home and said our goodbyes to all the men. They were sad to see us go and hugged Vertus and me repeatedly. I promised to speak with them again and moreover to ensure that I stayed in close contact.

During the flight home, I had so much on my mind. The trip to Indiana was more successful than I could have ever dreamed. I had the majority of my questions answered and more information than I thought possible. There was one question that still remained. I wanted to know if what happened at Lyles Station was an isolated case or was there record of other experiments. I recalled the story as relayed by the men at Lyles about Attorney McGee's insinuation that experiments may have been more commonplace than previously thought.

So by the time I returned home, my curiosity was peaked. I turned to the Internet, where a headline caught my eye—"The Ringworm Children: How the Israeli Government Irradiated 100,000 Israeli Kids." I was mystified by what this could mean. Like a mouse following a trail of cheese, I followed the links to the story.

It was a documentary filmed in Israel that contained reported facts that appear to have been confirmed by the Israeli government. The story discloses wrongdoings by the United States (U.S.) Military, charging that Israel, in collaboration with the U.S., experimented on 100,000 Moroccan children, refugees from North Africa, Asia and the Middle East. The film reported that the experiments involved massive levels of radiation, 35,000 times the acceptable level. In my mind's eye I saw the words of the Lyles Station children superimposed over what I read. This grabbed my attention in a big way. I searched for a reason to dismiss this as a hoax.

I ordered a copy of the film and watched it myself. The documentary reported that three hundred million Lira (billions in today's dollars) was paid in exchange for the experiments. To understand the magnitude of the payments, the entire budget for the state's health ministry was only 60 million Liras annually. The film disclosed facts that were later confirmed as true by the Israeli parliament.

The film explained that the world's reaction to the U.S. action, dropping the atomic bomb on Hiroshima and Nagasaki in 1945, was primarily unfavorable. At home, the U.S. Congress passed new laws halting the misuse of radiation. No one was angrier at halting than the U.S. Army, who at the time was allegedly in full development of an even more powerful weapon referred to as the "Mother Load," many times stronger than the atomic bomb.

The film added that the timing of the ban would have hurt America's atomic program, one that still required more testing and therefore needed to find subjects elsewhere. By 1948, Israel had begun functioning as a state and needed money. The U.S. Army provided the machines. In 1951, the director general of the Israeli Health Ministry, Dr. Chaim Sheba, flew to America and returned to Israel with seven x-ray machines, used for the experiments.

To fool the Moroccan parents, their children were taken away on supposed school trips. Parents were later told the x-rays were a treatment for scalpel ringworm. Almost unanimously, parents revolted, knowing their children had no ringworm. Up to ten thousand (10,000) children soon died after their doses, while others developed cancer that killed thousands more. The film alleges that some victims were shipped to the U.S. in cages for further observation and study. Victims suffered from such ailments as chronic headaches and cancers of the head, throat and brain.

One scene described a bearded man hunched over, walking the streets. "I'm in my fifties and everyone thinks I'm in my seventies," he states. A Moroccan lady described the after effects of deadly radiation administered. In a sorrowful voice, she said, "They brought us in lines, shaved our heads then smeared us with burning gel."

A technician admitted she was one of those who pulled the switch, administering the radiation to children. She cried, as she relayed that she did not understand the scope of what she was doing. She added, “I was told I was doing a good thing by helping to remove ringworm. If I knew what dangers the children were facing, I would never have cooperated, never!”

"The Ringworm Children" won awards at Jewish and Israeli film festivals. The story, in ways, is similar to that of Lyles Station though occurring a quarter of a century later. I was impacted by what I learned and I wanted Vertus to know. When I told him there might have been other victims of radiation poisoning, he cried, never dreaming that others could have suffered just as he, and even died during the experiments.

For the first time, I sensed Vertus speaking to me in grim detail about his possible fate when he said, “Wilbert, my condition could become cancerous and eventually kill me…I could die.” I also had that fear, but I didn’t have the courage to share it. Even then, instead of acknowledging he was right, I responded, “Vertus you’re as stubborn as an ox, cancer doesn’t want you.” But in reality it was I, kicking something down the road that needed to be dealt with. Losing Vertus would be very hard for me to accept.

During those moments when it looked as though I was organizing a pity party, Vertus would express words of comfort such as, “No matter the transgressions prevailed against me, it is more important that I react with a higher consciousness. My heart must react with room to forgive.”

I took the night off from research and went to the Karaoke Lounge with my wife and a couple of family members. Just having returned from Indiana, they were anxious to hear about my discoveries. There was one song made popular by the Staple Singers entitled *I’ll Take You There* that I listened to closely. The song spoke of heaven as a place where no one cried or worried. I knew this would one day be Vertus’ reward.

In 1951, Dr. Sheba returned from the U.S. with the above machine, one of seven allegedly given him by the U.S. Army. The machine delivered deadly radiation to treat ringworm that parents swore never existed. Photos taken from the above referenced documentary.

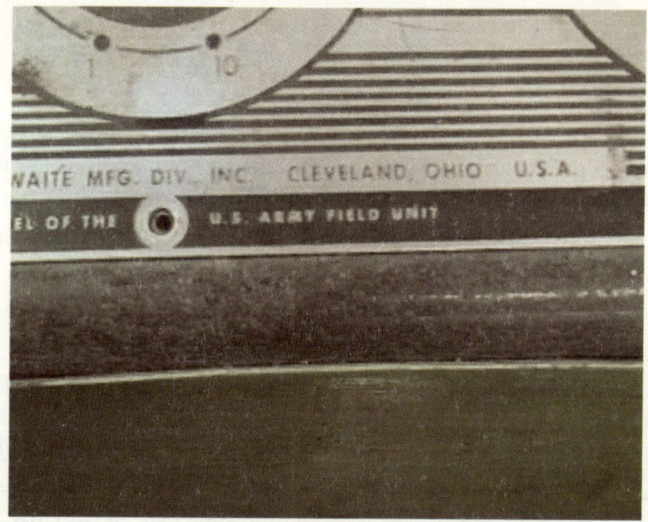

Another photo taken from the documentary shows the identification label taken from a machine once alleged to be the property of the U.S. Army Field Unit.

LINCOLN HIGH SCHOOL

After taking some time to organize my research and discussions, I realized that an important part of Vertus' story was missing. I needed to gather information about his teen and high school years. I called him and asked if we could return to taping in the weeks that followed. He agreed.

During one of his visits to my office the following week, Vertus brought books and paraphernalia from his high school years. I asked him to tell me more about them and he replied, "Well, I brought them so you could see for yourself." And then he shared that in 1937, at age 15, he and his family moved from Lyles Station to nearby Princeton. The family took residence on North Race Street, directly across from Abraham Lincoln High School. Segregated, like the school in Lyles Station, Lincoln High sat four miles to the east and educated ninth through twelfth graders.

Earliest known photo of Lincoln High School Progressive Reading Club under the instruction of G. H. Brown, second-row-center. To his left stands instructor Nora Craig. (Photo circa 1914)

This corner street sign was located just outside Vertus' residence. Pictured in the background is the roofline of the then family residence. The high school existed just four blocks from the all White Princeton High School. Both schools opened their doors to a street named Race. Lincoln High sat on the corner of Race and Walnut Street. (Photo 2006)

The Lincoln High School basketball team from 1941.

Lincoln High football team had eleven players, the required number needed to play both offense and defensive. (Photo 1941)

Vertus was small in stature and somewhat shy. He said, "I enjoyed playing games such as chess, checkers and dominoes. I liked girls but didn't have the confidence to interact with any beyond familiar ties and platonic friendships. I grew tired of the stares and constant inquiries about my head. I had a close-knit circle of friends who always looked out for me." The loss of skin color and the burn mark etched in an almost straight line across his forehead was obvious. Vertus was denied a waiver from rules forbidding the wearing of a hat while on school grounds, so he suffered through the embarrassment.

While a junior he obtained a part time job. He worked for the owner of the ice plant evenings from 4 to 8 pm. He did odd chores, including mowing the lawn. For months he considered buying a hair wig and secretly researched the subject. Information was scarce but he managed to scour the library for anything about false hair. He told no one about this passion or how deep it ran.

Then, fortune smiled. There was an old man who visited the ice plant owner's home. He sat on the porch talking with the owner while Vertus cut the grass. The visitor noticed that Vertus always wore a hat and from what he could see, he assumed Vertus had no hair. Vertus said, "The man usually sipped a cool beverage and appeared to have once been the victim of a fire—his face, neck and hands were badly discolored. I wanted to befriend him." And so Vertus did.

The old man seemed compassionate; however, it was Vertus who broached the subject of his condition and cause. The old man told about a fire that severely burned his upper torso, head and hands leaving him scarred and deformed. The man openly admitted to Vertus that he had since wore a wig. Vertus was intrigued. He told me, "I wanted to see his wig up close, touch it and feel its texture, but I was afraid to ask permission to touch it." But the old man somehow already knew of Vertus' desire.

Vertus said, "Over the next few weeks I threw him every question that came to mind, and he answered every one of them." The old man usually arrived about the time he thought Vertus might arrive. Eventually he shared enough trust that he told him, "I've saved enough to buy my wig." The old man was not surprised and seemed to understand perfectly how Vertus felt.

That day the old man removed his wig and allowed Vertus to handle it. He not only closely examined the wig but also got a chance to see the man up close without it. He saw the details of his injuries. Vertus described the moment, "I was looking at him as though looking into a mirror." While they didn't really resemble each other, it was their yearning for improvement that made them identical twins.

As Vertus told this story I was reminded of an old song made famous by the Ink Spots about the same time this incident occurred. The song is entitled *We Three.* Lyrics described three close companions who found themselves always together. The lonely threesome was named Echo, Shadow and Me! Perhaps the wig was Vertus' *Echo* and *Shadow* together, a component necessary to make him appear whole.

Vertus purchased a wig with savings earned from his work at odd jobs. His family was deeply touched by his tenacity and strong desire even at age fourteen. They hoped that in a small way the wig would help to hide the awful effects of the experiment. The entire community supported his new look. Vertus became a happier student and earned the second highest grade point average among his fellow classmates.

Vertus, at age 16, poses with his father shortly following the purchase of his first wig. The neighborhood bullies had either vanished or experienced a change of heart. Kids never knew that during the times Vertus' hat was snatched and flung, there also flew with his hat a portion of his broken heart. But all was so different now.

A proud 18 year-old Vertus wearing his wig and fancy Fedora during his senior year. This was his personality photo during graduation proceedings. (Photo 1941)

Vertus completed high school with honors. In his scrapbooks were the original programs he maintained since the 1940s for each of the events identified below. Included in the memory book were thoughts expressed by teachers and classmates alike, all wishing him well. I recorded events taken from programs dated May 12, 13, 20, 25 and 26, 1941. Below is a chronology of those events.

Monday, May 12, 1941

The school hosted a junior-senior reception in the auditorium. The cost of admission was 25 cents. Here seniors handed the torch to the underclassman as it was traditionally done since the school's inception. Vertus stated, "I recall this program and how we were so happy to be graduating."

Tuesday, May 13, 1941

The senior prom was held in the auditorium. This event cost one dollar per couple and commenced from 9pm till 1am. The junior class was always invited to bolster attendance. Vertus said, "Each of us received a small lead pencil attached to a dance card to record the song and who we danced with." Vertus kept the original pencil attached to the now 70-year-old dance card, never written on. The card was left blank. It was sad to imagine Vertus not having a single dance the entire evening.

Tuesday, May 20, 1941

The graduates were honored at Olive Branch Baptist Church. The program was a morning filled with breakfast and inspirational songs. Vertus recalled, "The minister described us graduates as men and women. That was the first time I was ever called a man."

Sunday, May 25, 1941

The Baccalaureate service was held in the Lincoln High School gymnasium beginning at 2 pm. Vertus said, "That day I committed my life to be a spiritual guide for myself and others."

Monday, May 26, 1941

At 8 pm, the school gymnasium hosted its commencement exercise. The class motto read "Today Decides Tomorrow." Vertus talked for hours about these special events, many times laughing and joking about what those years meant to him.

Vertus attended Lincoln High School from 1937 to 1941.

Above, Vertus arrives at school alongside fellow classmates.
(Photo circa 1940)

A STEP TOWARDS DIGNITY

Again I found myself at the Karaoke Lounge listening to a song that reminded me of Vertus. I thought about him yearning for the chance to work and be received as normal as everyone else. Reflections unveiled during the performance of a song recorded in the early 1960s by Sam Cooke. A patron performed the song entitled, *A Change Is Gonna Come.* I could imagine Vertus feeling this way. Luckily, there were big changes on the horizon that would enhance the way he felt about himself.

After graduation, Vertus chose not to attend college because it meant entering an even larger institution, compared to high school, subjecting him to larger degrees of embarrassment and ridicule. Upon graduation he was ordered by the local military draft board to report for a physical. Both he and his brother reported as ordered. They were examined by doctors then were asked questions about their heads. Following the examination doctors classified them as unfit. Vertus said, "Even the military didn't want us." With this rejection in mind, Vertus wanted to leave Princeton, but was not quite sure how to do so or where to go.

He had a friend whose father worked for the railroad. As a benefit, that family received travel passes and often chose to vacation in California. When the family returned to Princeton, the friend described California in the grandest of terms. He highlighted mountains with peaks touching the clouds and shared stories about the roar of the mighty Pacific Ocean. He touted California as another world. He told Vertus about seeing Negroes working everywhere.

Vertus had an aunt residing in California but at the time didn't think much about it. As a recent high school graduate, he believed doors would open for him in Princeton but he found there was no work. He stated, "I wanted more than a domestic job working around somebody's house." After a few months, he changed his mind and decided to leave Princeton. He thought a larger city would offer greater options. Vertus also had an aunt living in Chicago that he chose to contact for help. She responded with an offer of room and board.

Vertus was excited and boarded a bus, Chicago-bound. But when he got there he found the job situation was the similar to Princeton. Vertus said, "I got up at sunrise and searched for work until sunset. I walked all day with no success." He soon realized that Chicago was not the answer. He was so discouraged that he considered returning to Indiana. But just before acting on his thought, he learned about jobs offered in California as a result of the war effort. Vertus heard there were jobs for Negroes engaged as shipbuilders.

As luck would have it, Vertus had an excellent relationship with his aunt residing in the Los Angeles area. He immediately contacted her. Like before, this aunt was also eager to help him. Within days Vertus boarded a train for California.

Vertus stated, "In California, I landed my first real job working for the government as a pipe fitter's helper. The job included benefits and production bonuses. I earned sixty-five cents ($.65) per hour, well above the minimum wage of forty-three cents ($.43)." Vertus was proud of his new status and wrote home frequently to assure family that all was well. When the war ended in 1945, the news was considered both good and bad. Good that the war was over, but shipbuilding was no longer critical. Vertus was unfortunately forced back amongst the ranks of the unemployed.

He learned that a local Catholic school in East Los Angeles was looking for a janitor. Vertus applied but didn't believe he had much chance of success because he was not Catholic, a prerequisite for the job. During the job interview, he was asked about his religion. Vertus was honest, stating his membership in the Methodist Church. But the interview went better than he thought. He was offered the job on one condition. He had to convert to the Catholic religion.

Vertus kept his end of the bargain. For years, it meant he would practice two faiths, Catholic at dawn on Sunday and Methodist the remainder of the day. This was a testament to his commitment to the school. He said, "I did it for the job at first then I really learned to love the school and the students. I worked 5 ½ hours each day, beginning at 3:30 pm." Vertus maintained that shift for more than twenty years.

During this time, he fell hard for a girl that attended the Methodist church named Marguerite Bell. The two dated, spending countless hours playing dominoes, bowling and roller-skating. Vertus described their guiding foundation as spiritual. Together they attended both the morning and evening services while members of the same usher board. He said, "When Sunday night rolled around I wanted to get off my feet after standing and greeting parishioners all day long."

But the love affair with Marguerite did not last. Vertus was sad as he described the hesitancy on his part. He said, "I never truly accepted her love and devotion because I feared she would never accept me—I mean, the ugliness of what I was hiding under my wig." I was so touched by his words. I felt the high cost he paid for feeling inadequate.

Marguerite never saw Vertus without his wig and based upon what I heard, she faithfully awaited the moment he would trust her and show what he was hiding. Vertus feared the day of reckoning. So he pushed her away, believing Marguerite was too good to be true. He said, "I feared she would leave me if ever faced with the truth. This fear was never far away and subsequently, I never fully committed to our relationship." Vertus lost her either way. He found that gifts of candy, perfume and jewelry were not enough. Marguerite wanted his trust.

Vertus said, "I deeply regretted pushing aside the only woman I ever loved. I somehow knew there would never be another Marguerite." And Vertus was right. He never married or had children.

Marguerite Bell. (Photo 1945)

Vertus was completely devoted to his work. He interviewed for an additional job at the Los Angeles County Hospital. His intent was to remain loyal to the school that gave him an opportunity when others would not. When hired, he would work for the county during morning hours. He worked this additional job for over forty years.

Vertus received special recognitions over his career for incredible achievements, such as never missing a single day of work. By the time he retired, he had completed two careers, never in twenty years at the school, or forty years at the hospital, did he ever miss a single workday. He eventually was forced to resign the school job due to mounting responsibilities that accumulated over the decades he worked at the hospital, which required Vertus to frequently arrive early and stay later.

As Vertus shared this part of his life, I realized this was happening about the time I first entered grade school, five years old, the same age as Vertus at the time of the experiments. I challenged myself to compare my life at age five, recalling my most traumatic first grade moment then contrasting it to the experiments.

The worst thing I could recall was when my teacher asked our class what we wanted to be when we grew up. When my turn came, I responded, "I want to be a cowboy." I can't imagine what prompted my interest in that profession other than the recent Christmas gift from my parents: boots, guns, holsters, and a cowboy hat. My fellow classmates burst out in laughter over the thought of a Negro cowboy. Their reactions hurt me deeply, but it was nothing compared to Vertus. As I drew this comparison, my already gigantic appreciation for him grew even greater. I realized that Vertus was so damaged at age five that it ultimately defined and shaped who he became.

He learned to excel, becoming so driven that he was compelled to live life only one way. Perhaps that's why he never missed a single day of work and acquired a huge real estate portfolio. Maybe what we describe as overachievement was simply the norm for Vertus. I believe that while our culture was teaching Vertus that boys and men must be strong and not cry or show compassion, Vertus was choosing to channel his energy toward working extra hard. Maybe it made him in some way normal and his work ethic became his identity. It taught him to charge forward through life, never stopping, until the day he entered my office with the words, "I'm tired."

Here top row center, one cannot avoid noticing the thinly built Vertus wearing a wig. Employees wore daily uniforms consisting of matching khaki shirt and pants. Thirty-nine men and sixty-one women made up the Housekeeping Division. (Photo 1950)

At age five along with my brother Eddie, age four, glowing in our Christmas outfits. (Photo 1955)

Vertus shared that he was never completely comfortable during his working career. There was frequent pain and gossipers concocting all sorts of tales about why he wore a wig. Some accounts were deeply sinister while others were nothing short of bizarre. The most common description called him homosexual, defining his hair as part of an out of control life style. Others identified him as the victim of a brutal beating at the hands of a robber. Vertus never addressed the myths. He was a sharp dresser, never afraid of bright colors. He owned four different wigs over his years and hid his sadness underneath them all.

By age fifty Vertus had received numerous promotions resulting in greater responsibility. He used his earnings and excellent credit record to acquire real estate, ultimately owning 28 properties in the greater Los Angeles area. He had a reputation for giving marginal renters a break and seldom paid a price for his generosity. Vertus never boasted about his wealth and kept busy working at his properties while serving as president of three homeowner associations—The Chapman Manor, Monticello Manor and the Mendocino Villa association. But the largest part of his life was his church. Vertus stated, "I served the Lord faithfully as my repayment for his many blessings."

Vertus poured his heart into the many roles at the church. He was an active member of the trustee board, finance committee, cathedral choir, and men's chorus...all at the same time. He faithfully donated, once saying to the congregation, "When I die you will see my love for our church."

Vertus as seen in the church directory dressed in a jacket purchased from the local thrift store. The jacket became one of his favorites.

Doctors Looking Under A Rug

Decades later

Since he was a teenager, Vertus wore a wig. Now, at age 81, his wound has deteriorated and the wig became too heavy to rest against it. The wig came to cause him severe pain, and he was forced to abandon wigs forever. One could imagine his uneasiness when considering what could replace it. He settled on a simple beanie, which he owned in a variety of colors.

The wound now emitted a constant burning that would strike frequently, with greater intensity. Lesions continued to resurface, as they had since age fifty. Numerous medical specialists examined Vertus, but none were able to help. Their reactions were identical, each in disbelief. They identified Vertus' wound as an ulcerated sore brought about by excessive exposure to radiation. Doctors warned him to have timely screenings for cancer and if it were ever detected, Vertus was warned never to undergo radiation treatments. The same radiation used to kill cancer cells is the same radiation responsible for the original horror in 1927. Therefore, radiation therapy would never be an option.

Vertus was also warned that his wound could worsen, but nobody ever forecasted the possibility of his skull caving in. Vertus said, "I have been betrayed so often by the promise of tomorrow's cure." But in spite of past medical failures, he somehow remained optimistic. I recall hearing him say, "One day I will peel this thing from my head as though peeling an orange."

John Waldron, a general practitioner, was Vertus' medical doctor. Dr. Waldron first saw Vertus for unrelated, flu-like symptoms, never knowing about his scalp. Vertus arrived at his first appointment with Dr. Waldron, wearing a wig then eventually, just a beanie. Vertus never removed either covering or volunteered any information. The doctor never saw his wound until 2005 when Vertus developed headaches. The pain prompted a visit to the doctor at which time Vertus removed his beanie. Dr. Waldron was surprised!

The doctor determined that Vertus' wound had advanced to the point of needing a specialist immediately and he submitted the appropriate referral. His case brought together specialist from a number of medical disciplines that developed a team approach to help him. Individually none of the specialist had a solution but they hoped to work together to develop one.

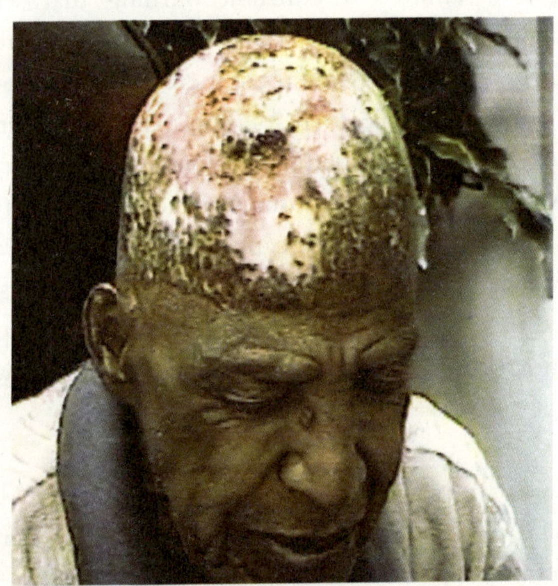

The last photo taken before the first hole in Vertus' skull appeared. Vertus was no longer able to wear a wig due to the pain caused by its weight.

Dr. John Waldron, a very competent and compassionate doctor that ultimately became a friend to Vertus. In some ways these two friends drew a mutual comfort from each other.

The following week Vertus was scheduled with doctors to receive an MRI (Magnetic Resonance Imaging) exam, a medical procedure most commonly used to visualize the structure and functions of the body. It would assist doctors with useful neurological (brain) and oncological (cancer) analysis. This was a tool necessary to pull together details of his condition. It was hoped there could be a unique repair and recovery plan devised for Vertus.

The MRI confirmed the presence of cancer cells but ruled out any advancement into the brain, a sort of good news-bad news scenario. It did create a sense of urgency that the cancer was growing dangerously close to Vertus' brain. If this growth remained unchecked, the cancer could easily consume his brain and cause death. Frequent biopsies were suggested, as many as twelve during the most recent twelve-month period. Surgery was assumed the best hope to remove the affected tissues, followed by aggressive reconstruction procedures. It would be risky at best, but a risk Vertus said, "I am very willing to take."

Dr. Nichols was the lead specialist that made up the tumor board. We were told the board wished to meet with Vertus for evaluation purposes, with a view towards plastic and neurosurgery. We were given a well-awaited appointment. When Vertus learned about the plan, he spoke of a dream he had. He said, "Wilbert I'm going to lose this dreadful thing from my head. I may actually get my chance to peel my orange." He next joked, "Maybe the procedure will include a finish coat of ready-plant hair to replace the hair taken from me 80 years ago."

In response I smiled affectionately, convinced I was hearing the five-year-old boy speaking out again. I tried to be as encouraging as possible, but my biggest fear was the potential for letdown if they found they could not help Vertus. This, I kept to myself.

During our visit, we saw nine physicians, each classified as a specialist. We sat around a conference table where Dr. Nichols led the discussion. There were specialists from the two major university hospitals and the remainder from Vertus' health insurance carrier. Seriously focused, this group seemed void of any laughter or idle chat. There was a spoken reminder of the meeting's purpose followed by a review of the images of Vertus' head that filled the table. Electronic viewers were used to show the images.

Each specialist took their turn at questioning Vertus and examining his wound. Vertus told the wound's history and described the pain and sensitivity he lived with daily. They were extremely careful not to leave Vertus with false expectations. But in spite of it all, Vertus had his dream and assumed this was the time for his dream's fulfillment. He wanted this dream to become truth. When the meeting adjourned, I asked Dr. Nichols if we could speak privately.

We stepped a few feet down the hallway where the doctor said, "You know your father is in a very critical state. I responded, "Yes I know." He went on to tell me that he and his associates would continue meeting and reach their conclusion. He said we would be notified to come back for a follow-up. He asked that I not get my hopes up yet. I told the doctor that I clearly understood. When I noticed Vertus was coming our way, I cut the conversation and wished the doctor a good day. Dr. Nichols in turn thanked us both for coming in.

Understandably the return ride home was emotional. Vertus told me, "This is probably my last lifeline, my final opportunity for help." Vertus felt that if a cure were not found by the incredible amount of specialty and wisdom around that table, if they could not help him, it was safe to assume he was beyond medical help.

After several minutes of riding silently, we began to dialogue again. Vertus offered a prayer that God would guide the doctors during their decision and began thanking God for allowing him to live this long. This was a heart-filled moment. I did not look in his direction fearing he would make me cry. I was simultaneously on my own verge of joy and sorrow. If the doctors could help him it would be incredibly joyous and if they could not, it might be all Vertus could bear. I knew it was not wise to get my hopes up, but how could I not.

I thought about Dr. Nichols' reference to Vertus as my father. For the first time I realized that Vertus' condition was similar to that of my biological father. I recall the sorrow of hearing bad news, the misfortune experienced while hearing the voice of the attending physician describe my biological father's fragile prognosis for survival. Words like, "We have over three thousand patients admitted and I would estimate your father as one of the ten most critical." Flashbacks like these began to occur frequently.

Within the context of this puzzle, there were now three. It consisted of Vertus, my father and me. Because my dad was the victim of a homicide, he was taken without warning and my closure with him was pending. Imaginably, I was creating closure through Vertus by my display of love and companionship, being present during medical appointments and being that sounding board during times of deep meditation. This was replacing hollow feelings of helplessness that I felt during my father's passing. It was becoming clearer that through Vertus I was saying goodbye and expressing love and compassion I never said to my dad. I appreciated the man God granted me, he was like a father.

A Bubble Broken

Approximately two weeks had passed and today was the follow-up visit with the specialists. I awakened after barely any sleep in anticipation of the news this day would bring. Vertus was filled with optimism and felt today his prayer would be answered. Vertus prayed, "Lord if it's your will." And unlike the farmers who prayed for rain and did not carry an umbrella, Vertus had his suitcase packed with pajamas, robe, slippers, and toothpaste. The case was placed near the front door, a testament to his faith.

I drove through the morning traffic—an hour and a half to travel the eighteen-mile route. There was little dialogue between us; we both were nervous. I could not help but wonder how many times previously Vertus has arrived at a medical facility, only to have his hopes shattered.

We entered the oncology department and were instructed to sit in the patient waiting area then eventually redirected to a small office. The office contained a desk and two accompanying side chairs designated for patients. This was a far cry from the larger conference room that earlier seated the group of specialist. I anticipated the same group would be present to discuss plans for surgery. Oh well, maybe I had watched too many episodes of *General Hospital* and this is how it's really done.

Minutes later, Dr. Nichols entered, sat down and following brief salutations began to speak. "Mr. Hardiman, as you know we conducted the MRI that allowed us to more closely evaluate you. Unfortunately, we found a few unsuspected outcomes." Those words were enough for me to sense where this was likely headed. I cringed and cried out to myself, "Oh no!"

The doctor continued saying that the neurology department expressed major concerns about the cancerous target area resting dangerously close to Vertus' brain. This in itself presented severe risk. And if they could remove it, there was no way to close the gaping hole in his head. I learned they came together primarily to see and confer as a group that nothing was missed. They concluded after we left that there was nothing else they could do.

It was another let down in the path to Vertus' broken heart. For the first time I was sure that death would soon take my dear friend. I placed my hand on his shoulder and saw the tears filling his eyes. He could not stop them nor did he attempt to hide them. I could hear his fragile heart breaking and God only knows how many times that heart had previously required mending. There was no untapped panacea, magic bean or mystical arrow left to employ. There were only sessions remaining with his Creator, completely private and void of man's capacity to intervene.

Vertus and I discussed the Tumor Board's decision that he was beyond their help. (Photo 2007)

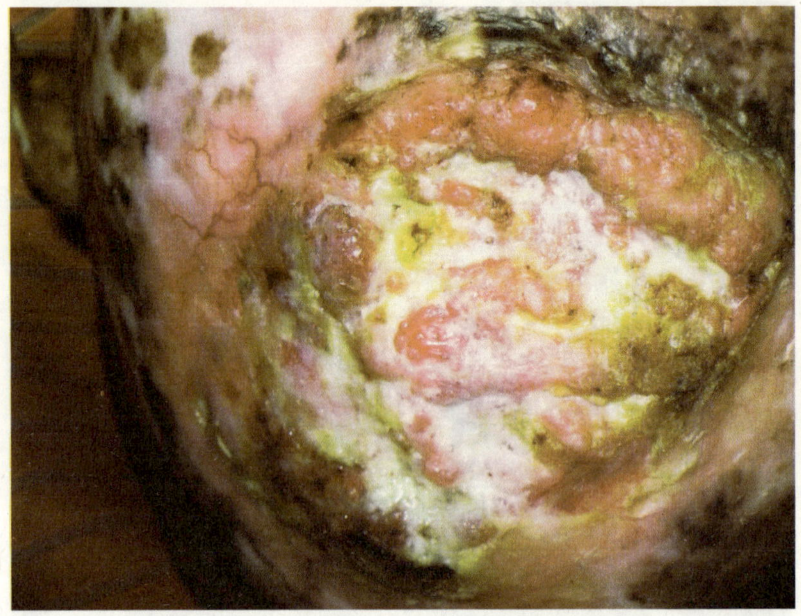

This is the top view of Vertus' wound as seen by the nine specialists. (Photo 2007)

In Preparation

Vertus was now thinking about and preparing for death. He was sitting at the dining room table and said he had questions about his net worth. He told me he was making plans and needed to get his business straight. I told him this was an excellent idea and reminded him that it was never too soon. I answered questions about his developing a living trust and will. He decided to hire an attorney to develop both.

For the first time he confided in me his chosen beneficiaries, those worthy of receiving the fruits of his life's work. I listened but had no illusion he was seeking my opinion. The decision was his and his alone. He said he planned to leave 75% of his wealth to his church. The remaining portion was to be gifted to his favorite charity. Vertus mentioned that he wanted to leave something for me but I insisted that he not do that. I told him that he should continue on his current path. He designated financial gifts to some of his family members and selected an attorney and executor to supervise his wishes.

His net worth was unbelievably eight million dollars. He confirmed that he had no college education and swung a mop many of his work years. He told me, "You'd be surprised just how much you can achieve when you save and don't waste your money." I could figure out a portion of his financial formula, knowing the basic drill, but must admit that I never really understood how the numbers netted out. I was certain that his retirement checks and rental income were received monthly and there were very few bills, if any, to pay. I also knew that his real estate properties were owned free and clear.

I commented, "Coming from very humble beginnings, it's quite an accomplishment to acquire such wealth." Vertus took little credit for his achievements, handing the glory to God as he stated, "God has blessed me." Vertus was not caught in the web of self-promotion, unwilling to accept praise.

Vertus resided in a condo located on the second floor of a two-story complex. A similar unit located on the first floor was offered for sale at $287,000. Vertus mentioned, "I think I'll make an offer. There will come a day when I will not have the strength to climb stairs. I need to buy that first floor unit. Wilbert, what do you think?" I told him the price seemed fair and perhaps he should make an offer. All things were considered and escrow was opened.

He didn't apply for a bank loan, I assumed because he had funds in time certificate accounts or some other form of savings, even though I never saw or heard about such an account. But within weeks my answer came in the form of a rare occurrence.

It was the day before the close of escrow when Vertus asked that I stop by his home. He welcomed me that morning and mentioned that he needed help with something. Sure I told him and asked what it was. He explained that funds were needed by escrow to complete the condo purchase. Escrow required about three hundred thousand dollars for closing. I said no problem but wondered why this was seemingly so complex. Why did Vertus need my help? I waited for the other shoe to fall.

He moved toward the door and gestured with a nod of his head for me to follow. We walked towards the rear of the property to a row of garages. Vertus searched for the entry key among a huge ring of keys from all his properties. At the door were two padlocks, each securing a separate side of the door. Vertus opened one then the other; slid open the slide lock before raising the door. Once inside, he turned on a light before closing the door behind us.

It still had not registered with me what was going on but when it did it hit like a ton of bricks. In fact, I recall the thought, April Fools on you too Vertus Hardiman...I'm not going to be the brunt of your joke. But Vertus was not smiling. He was serious.

He opened the drawer to a 1960's style metal file cabinet. I saw the secrecy, the closing of the door and his looking around to assure privacy, but still had no clue what was occurring. He opened the drawers and removed several metal boxes. I remarked jokingly, "Vertus you handle those like they're gold. What's in there, money?" Vertus responded with a nod, yes! In disbelief, I knew this was no prank. This was an improvised safe!

We took the boxes back to his unit and placed them on the living room table. I was interested in seeing just how much money was really there while wondering how much more did we leave in the garage. I cannot put into words just how astonished, yet humbled I felt, at the thoughts of just how much Vertus obviously trusted me, but at the same time I thought he was nuts!

The cash was bound in bundles of $5,000. We must have removed about 60 bundles before transferring the load into paper bags. Vertus didn't seem the least bit uneasy leading me to believe he had completed this type of cash transaction before. It was nothing short of incredible to imagine the potential damage an ember of fire could do to the garage's contents. It was inconceivable to realize just how much Vertus depended upon an old file cabinet or on the flip side, just how little he trusted banks.

I telephoned the local bank manager to alert him of our bringing in approximately $300,000 in cash for deposit. During the short trip to the bank, I was uneasy, frightened to be more precise. We didn't speak a word during the short trip, but Vertus seemed calm. Not I—I had the jitters. I felt like an un-armored transport guard.

I have known the branch manager for years, and at my expense, today particularly, I was the object of his quick wit. We sat in a conference room and verified the transaction while I was being teased about ties to the mafia, drugs and money laundering. Needless to say, we conducted the transaction and converted the money into a cashier's check that we took over to escrow.

SEVEN MONTHS LATER

It was the holiday season and Vertus was visiting my office more frequently, about twice a week. He would drop in just to chat for a while wanting nothing in particular. His loneliness was more obvious. I didn't always have time, but I knew Vertus relied so much upon me. The day before Thanksgiving, I called asking if he made plans for the holiday. He said no. I didn't want him spending the Thanksgiving holiday alone and was pleased when he accepted my invitation and would be with us on the holiday.

I'd never know how he was feeling from one day to the next. Some days were better than others. On bad days he couldn't do very much because of headaches or other ailments. On Thanksgiving morning I drove to his home, picked him up, then drove to a gathering hosted by my brother. We enjoyed our feast, but above all, gave thanks for all we had.

Central to that theme was Vertus and the thought of our many blessings and just how much we take for granted. Vertus had a good time laughing and joking with my family. He laughed at their stories, especially the ones about me being a stern big brother. He also took the time to share his love for God and his church and how much he valued our friendship. My mother, along with Vertus, led the evening prayer. We all really loved him.

Vertus posed on Thanksgiving Day with my mother D'Evelyn and sister Joyce Smith.

At Christmas time it was customary for our office to decorate. That particular year we wanted to add something extra by inviting Vertus to participate. I was looking for any opportunity to include him when doing things that seemed small to us but loomed large in his world. More than anything I feared this could be his last Christmas with us. I wanted nothing in return from him for I had already received so much. Because of Vertus I was certain I was a better person.

I was reminded of the story of a young boy who complained of having no shoes. The following day the boy ran upon another his same age who had no feet. Astonished by what he saw, the boy vowed never again to complain and to give thanks for what he had. When I think of this story, I think of Vertus as the boy with no feet.

Vertus did not allow the experiment to become a source of anger. He made it clear, saying, "If my heart were filled with anger, there would be little room for love and without love, my prayers would not be answered." He went on by reciting this little poem that his mother taught him. "A chicken sets out to get even, while the old crow complains, but notice the eagle is so content, as he rises high in the sky above it all." (Author unknown)

Vertus and Kimberly share a joyous Christmas day moment. It was a happy day for Vertus.

One Hole Too Many

It was Sunday morning, and Vertus and I attended church. He did not join the choir that morning, unable to handle the rigors of singing. He was really missed. Whenever church members or community acquaintances and friends asked about him, I only told them so much; his secret remained safe. He did not break his silence regarding the experiments and his subsequent condition.

He continued to fear that those who professed love and friendship, would pressure him to show his wound if they knew of its existence. All his life he saw silence as the easier approach. I tried to change his mind, but he was steadfast and unwilling to compromise.

This particular Sunday at church, he had a great time. By special request, the choir sang his favorite songs and dedicated them in his honor. Most who knew him noticed a physical change. There was a slower pace about him, an obvious stagger with his walk. His steps were shorter. I'm certain he wanted to look strong but he would quickly say without hesitation, "I'm an old man now."

There were times when it was necessary for him to remain in bed due to ailments compounded by the cancer. After church, I offered our usual spot for lunch, but Vertus refused. He said he was tired from the morning's events and would rather go home to rest.

The following Wednesday I dropped by to check on him. Of all the days and hours we spent together, today was memorable. Vertus wore his customary beanie; this one was black. He sported a pair of fire-engine-red suspenders atop a multi colored shirt. I smile as I recollect that these colors did not come close to matching but nonetheless they were very spirited. I asked, "How are you feeling?'

Vertus replied, "I'm feeling pretty good Wilbert. I just thank God for each day I can get up and see daylight, because he didn't have to let me do it."

Total Praise sadly performed that Sunday without Vertus. (Photo 2007)

I responded, "What does that mean?" He replied, "That I have my health and strength…that I can see and hear…that I'm in my right mind." He then concluded, "Those are blessings…three blessings." I was speechless and motivated to change another part of my life. That was the last day I complained about things that I felt were not perfect. That was the single most important lesson I learned from him.

I knew he really wasn't feeling well but that response was typical Vertus, only wanting me to experience his brighter side. I thought about all the salutations heard daily by others, "I guess I'll make it," "Doing fair," "I'm so-so." Then I think of Vertus and, justifiably so, aspire to be like him.

Vertus said, "Since as early as I could remember, I wanted to be looked upon as a human being and not a monster." He asked me, "Could you imagine living life with the fear of being seen as you really are?" I answered, "No Vertus, not in my wildest dreams." He told me how he feared the question, "What happened to you?" He stated it would lead to someone requesting to see his wound, a request he would never grant. His words represented kindness and compassion, and I lovingly cared for him. Vertus allowed me the honor of looking beyond his wound, peering into his huge spirit. When I looked at him, I first saw his gigantic heart.

Vertus seated in my office praising life and acknowledging the many blessings he is so thankful for. (Photo 2006)

THE BREAKING POINT

I received a call at about 2 am. Whenever the telephone rings at that hour, one can assume the worst. I peered at the caller ID then quickly answered the phone. It was Vertus! Why was he calling now? I assumed a real emergency! My greeting was abrupt, "Vertus, what's wrong?" His agitated voice responded, "A piece of my skull has just cracked, Wilbert I have a hole in my head. My skull is breaking apart."

I couldn't understand what he meant. I asked him if he was sure. Vertus requested that I come over immediately. He said I was not going to believe what happened. I couldn't take him literally. How does your skull crack without it somehow being struck?

I arrived at his home within minutes. Vertus took me to his bathroom where I examined his head while he stared into the mirror. He held in one hand a pair of tweezers used as a pointing device and in the other hand was a mirror. From my vantage point, I could see it. It was easily visible, a hole in his skull. It was the height and width of a toothpick. My first thought was to call paramedics but Vertus stated he felt fine, nothing outside the ordinary.

He began giving the accounts leading to the discovery. He saw something just above his scalp. The protrusion was in the right frontal portion of his scalp. He chose to grab it with his fingers. It could not be removed and he could not feel it. He used a pair of tweezers to grip the item and pulled on it. When he did so it snapped! Vertus heard the break; the unforgettable echo was his bone snapping away. He assumed he was looking at his skull but in reality he was numb, mentally paralyzed by what was occurring.

There remaining was a sort of peephole that allowed one to plainly see into the inside of his head. This was one of the most shocking things I had ever had to absorb. At first, all I could do was just stand there and stare in the mirror at him. More than ever I was scared for Vertus, really scared, but I couldn't let him know it! Of all the challenges my friend faced, it was now exacerbated by a hole in his head!

I had difficulty processing my thoughts. What if water gets inside this hole? This situation brought to mind a prior discussion I had with Vertus a few months earlier when he told of a specialist, who, in the early 1980's, warned that one day he would wash his scalp and notice his skull breaking apart. This was a morbid thought at the time. And what if a piece of bone has fallen inside his head?

I took Vertus immediately to the Emergency Room (ER). While in route, neither of us spoke a word. I was now fully initiated as a part of his once private world. We were headed to see an ER doctor, who more than likely had never seen anything like this. Vertus laid his head against the headrest during the thirty-minute ride.

The doctor arranged for Vertus to receive the highest possible priority. Vertus wore his beanie, hiding any evidence of the trauma. The intake clerk shivered as I described his condition, curious as to how this could be possible. And oddly, Vertus showed no signs of discomfort. She never asked him to see the hole; instead, she called for a nurse. They immediately took Vertus into an observation room. Within minutes doctors walked in. They asked questions and pulled records reflecting Vertus' medical history. They asked if he was in pain and Vertus hung his head and answered no.

Vertus rested in the ER for the remainder of the night, awaiting the scheduled 7 am opening of the wound clinic. They continued to monitor his vitals and took plenty of x-rays to verify there was no bone fragment inside his skull. They calmed our fears of immediate danger.

I saw Vertus crumbling before my very eyes. Humans have seven (7) holes in their head, two ears, two nostrils, one mouth and two eye-sockets. Tragically, Vertus possesses an eighth hole. While his bed was wheeled to the clinic, he looked up at me and said "I guess you've never saw a man with a hole in his head!" "No," I replied, "I'm certain I never have."

THE WOUND CLINIC

The wound clinic expected us. By coincidence, we were scheduled to see Dr. Afram, someone I have known personally for 15 years. Dr. Afram is a neighbor that I met at an open house held at our local high school. Our sons were close friends and teammates on the school basketball team. I was glad to see him and even more pleased to know he would be the one supervising Vertus' care.

Dr. Afram evaluated Vertus and acted calmly, as though his condition was routine. I asked as he examined Vertus, had he ever seen anything like that? His response was "Yes." But I just couldn't believe that. I sensed the veteran doctor knew his positive words would go a long way to relieve Vertus' fear. Dr. Afram never stopped talking to Vertus and spoke about unrelated subjects. I'm sure this helped relax Vertus.

The doctor summoned his assistant and gave the order to prepare Vertus for cleaning and dressing. This bought us time to step into the hallway to chat. Once outside the room, Dr. Afram shook his head in disbelief. He confirmed he was doing what he could to soften the impact on Vertus. He asked if Vertus was a relative. He went on to say that he was very concerned about the opening and that his skull was so porous that the hole could likely open wider. He added that Vertus' mobility and independence could become severely compromised. He told me Vertus was entering his final stage of life.

I was moved by these words. Dr. Afram said he had devoted his career to preventing and healing wounds and had seen his share of tissue breakdown, and Vertus may be one of the worst he has witnessed. We kept the conversation brief so as not to evoke any additional fear in Vertus, then reentered the room.

Vertus usually relied upon me to do my share of talking when with doctors, but he always paid close attention while asking questions of his own. Strangely, today, he asked no questions. I'm certain it was a culmination of recent events with Dr. Nichols, and now Dr. Afram, that have Vertus completely overwhelmed. I asked Dr. Afram about the hole and the dangers of infection. I also asked what would happen if water or other contaminants entered his head. Dr. Afram said there was nothing to worry about, stating that water wouldn't hurt anything. He also said there was always a risk of infection. I asked if there was technology available to close the hole. Dr. Afram said nothing he was aware of. He again reminded me that the hole would likely get larger, as it subsequently did.

We left Dr. Afram with medications, dressings and information to care of his wound. On the way home Vertus said, "I'm so frustrated with decades of battling this. I am losing the battle to survive." I knew Vertus wanted and needed my support, and I was committed to being there. He asked me how long I could be counted on. I wasn't sure of the words to say, but I told Vertus I wasn't going anywhere, that I would be with him every step of the way.

THREE MONTHS LATER

For the months that followed, we returned to the wound clinic every few weeks for general status and follow-up. Vertus was no longer driving and relied heavily on others to get around. There was a longtime friend who we arranged to help manage his properties. He collected rents and coordinated needed repairs. He was an honest man that eventually moved into Vertus' spare bedroom. His contribution was timely.

As Dr. Afram predicted, the hole in Vertus' head became larger. His skull was cracking apart, and when measured in February 2007, the hole was four centimeters wide by four centimeters long. It had a depth of 2.5 centimeters, measured from the scalp's surface down to the dura mater, the outer most protective layer surrounding the brain and spinal cord.

Vertus described a cracking sound heard by the up and down pulsating beneath his skull. It would rise and fall, triggering movement near the area of broken skull. The movement caused a cracking sound that Vertus heard in response to every heartbeat. Vertus said, "The sound could easily drive you insane." There was no way to stop the cracking sound driven by his every heartbeat. While looking in the mirror, Vertus described what he saw in very harsh terms. He asked, "Look at me…I look like some monster from a horror movie! Don't I?"

I understood his reaction, but it disturbed me to hear him describe himself in such a way. I wanted Vertus to see the same things I saw, though I knew it was easier said than done. I went on to remind him of the richness that dwelled beneath the hole in his head. I took a few minutes to remind him of God, who made him in his image and to whom he chose to pray daily. He responded, "Yes I know, you are right." He whispered that he was thankful for living this long.

With each appointment, Vertus entered into a psychological holding pattern until Dr. Afram confirmed that the hole was not getting bigger nor the cancer advancing. One day, we learned it was not the hole in his head that was the most critical. Instead, it was the growing tumor that rested dangerously close to his brain. Vertus was dying and each remaining day was more precious than ever.

That evening I went to Karaoke and heard a song made popular by Ray Charles. The song *Georgia* found me deep into its lyrics as I envisioned the hole in Vertus' head. The hole was Vertus' symbol of Georgia. No matter the direction of the roads he traveled, that road always led back to the reality of his condition. Georgia was the wound he bore.

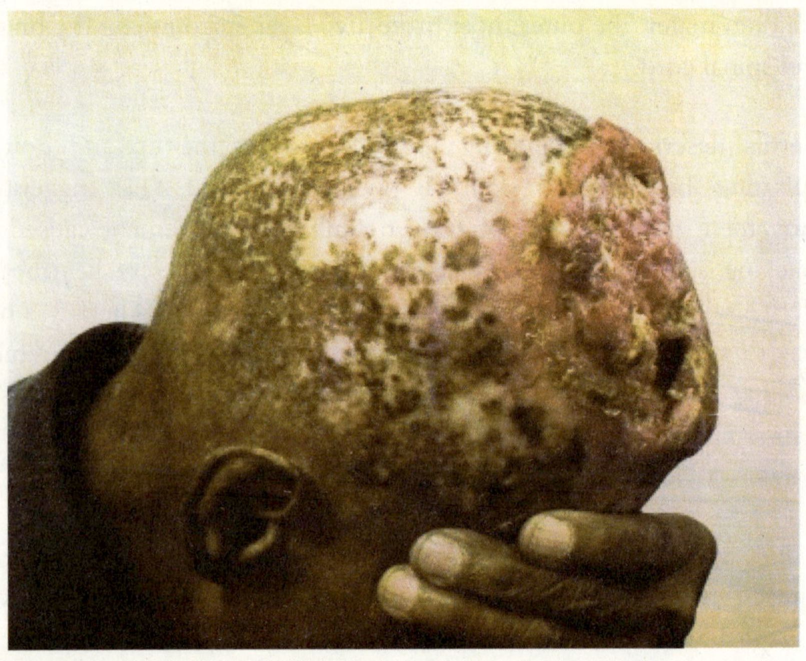

Vertus was deep in thought while we waited to be examined by Dr. Afram. I wondered what he was thinking. He wondered how long he could continue life's simple tasks, such as showering or preparing a simple meal. (Photo 2007)

Looking Over a Shoulder

Life moved on as Vertus sat and reminisced about his family in Indiana. Both his parents were deceased due to natural causes after surviving well into their nineties. His brother Melvin and sister Vera were in Indianapolis along with cousins Horace and Fuzz. Uncle Gletus continued to live in Lyles Station. They had no idea what was happening to Vertus and knew nothing about the hole in his head.

He never thought to travel anymore and when he wrote to them, his words never included his medical condition. The last time he traveled was the trip he and I took to Lyles Station. He didn't tell anyone, neither family or friend about his condition, preferring not to raise alarm.

As for me, it was times like this that I missed my dad. Sometimes when I saw Vertus' head I could not help but flashback to my father. It became impossible to easily separate the two traumas. I anguished for them both.

One day while leisurely recording Vertus' story, I asked him, "Are you angry with all the trauma this experience has caused you?" Vertus responded, "No! I learned a long time ago that you can't get ahead when trying to get even." I followed up, "Are you pleased with your life's work? If given the opportunity, what would you do differently?" He was silent for a minute. Then in a humbled way he simply said, "I did my best."

I asked about his prayers and the hope they would be answered. I wondered if his prayers in prior years and his prayers today were with equal intensity and meaning. I wanted to know if he felt ready to face judgment before the God we served. There were no surprises in any of his responses. He replied, "There is no difference in my prayer. If you are asking if I fear dying the answer is no. Of course, I made some mistakes that I would do differently if given the chance; but I believe I did well. It all rests with somebody bigger than you and I." At that point I turned off the recording.

In later reflections, I realized how extremely proud I was of Vertus. I thought of the thousands of employees that worked with and for him over the years. I wanted them to get a glimpse of him, the real Vertus Hardiman, without the wig or beanie. I wanted them to talk to him, to feel his truest glee and deepest pain. I wanted them to hear the whispering and the resulting laughter from the scores of jokes told throughout his lifetime. Perhaps too little too late, or maybe on the contrary it would be just enough to finally set the record straight.

I located former employees/colleagues from Vertus' days at county general hospital. Avanell Griffin, Geneva Hildreth and Robert Perry agreed to meet with me. In their own words, I would learn of the impact Vertus had on their lives.

Geneva hired Vertus and was instrumental in helping guide his career. She spoke of his unique ability to motivate and inspire others to greater heights. She remembered his encouraging words "Go for it," stating, "Just because you are a custodian does not mean you can't grow." She said, "Vertus forced those around him to dream."

Avanell stated, "He gave me the confidence that I did not have. I was a custodian and he inspired me to believe I could be a secretary. He encouraged me to believe that I could work in an office environment even though I functioned at the lowest level in the housekeeping department. It was because of that belief in me, that I grew, promoting to more senior assignments."

Robert chimed in, "We loved to work for him. He was never afraid to roll up his sleeves and be hands on, showing you a better way to do things." Robert continued with a story about Vertus, who asked him once what he aspired to be. Robert responded, "I want your job!" Vertus didn't flinch. He told Robert that was great and encouraged him that if he worked hard enough, there was a strong possibility he would get there. Remarkably, when Vertus was promoted, Robert was selected to replace him.

The mood was subdued when I shared with them the facts surrounding the experiments. I then disclosed the effects of the radiation on Vertus and the other victims, including photos of his wound. For the first time they were allowed to venture beneath the wig Vertus wore to work for forty years. They thought back and commented, "If those who treated him with such cruelty only knew Vertus was doing the best he could."

As I reflected on the many years Vertus interacted with his employees/colleagues, I'm reminded of memories both good and bad. I remembered a statement Vertus once said to me, no doubt making it easier to endure the more difficult times. "People will always talk about you, especially when they envy you and the life you live." Maybe, in reality, they saw Vertus as exemplary in his actions of kindness. Vertus was wise not to fight them; he obviously affected their lives while never allowing them to affect his.

"People will always talk about you, especially when they envy you and the life you live."

-Vertus

A Prayer Spoken

It was now becoming more difficult to schedule things with Vertus because of the unpredictability of his illness. He fought severe headaches and other distractions almost daily. His classification was critical and he was assumed in the worst imaginable pain. Drugs were prescribed that escalated into a formula of stronger and stronger, prescribed in greater dosages that resulted in serious side effects. If it wasn't constipation, it was nausea, or something more severe.

The medications also caused Vertus to withdraw by way of excessive sleep and loss of appetite. There was rapid weight loss coupled with weakness and depression. I had faith in the specialist treating him, but found it challenging to ensure Vertus used his medications responsibly. I prayed that my alarm was unwarranted, but in reality, the drugs caused him to sleep excessively and soon became his quintessential escape. I reminded Vertus that life was still worth enjoying and that he needed his strength and energy to survive it.

Unfortunately, the lure was too great and equally convenient, it was just easier to sleep the days away and forget about the man in his mirror. We were engaged in a tug of war with a newfound adversary. Vertus became very dependent on the medications. During his most vibrant times, Vertus weighed about 165 pounds, but now he weighed about 105. When we eliminated certain meds, he responded with greater alertness and energy, a more vibrant person. His appetite would improve and Vertus would eat to satisfy it. The main culprit was the drug Morphine, the one I came to refer to as the bully of the block.

During a lighter moment I sat at his bedside and reflected on the past. We discussed the female technician who gave him the radiation.

Vertus wondered how the ordeal affected her during her lifetime. He wondered if she had her own haunting dreams and prayed at her church alter for forgiveness. Vertus said, "Maybe she wanted the opportunity to tell me and the other victims how wrong the experiments were and how sorry she was to be a part of them."

Vertus told me things such as, "I know that girl very well. I have heard her voice throughout my entire life." But instead of hearing him speak his anger at her, he instead told me about the times he had prayed for her. Vertus added, "Just maybe at a point in time, she offered a similar prayer, asking for mercy from God and forgiveness from the victims she injured."

This was a very sad moment. We shared our concerns about his cancer. Vertus was frightened and told me as times before, that he didn't want me to abandon him. I was perhaps his closest link to earth and I patiently assured him he would not be alone. He had no children and no one who understood what he was going through, which was why I was so patient when responding to his fear of abandonment. Vertus enumerated the following worries:

- Losing his mind and living his remaining days in a vegetative state.
- Being kept alive by artificial means.
- Being abandoned by me before the very end of his life.
- Not be allowed to die while at home.

While continuing to ensure that all was in order, we went to the mortuary to make final arrangements. Vertus selected a huge mortuary that received on average, thirty cases a day. He brought with him a policy purchased years earlier. When I saw the statement of funeral goods and services, I saw that the policy paid a sum of $3391.00. Of course at one time this was quite adequate, but surely, given no inflation guard, it was a far cry less than required. On that day, Vertus made plans to pay the needed cash to supplement his insurance death benefit and gave me the following instructions:

- He wanted no funeral or any other type of public display.
- He wished not to be embalmed.
- He wanted to be wrapped in swaddling cloth.
- He wished to be buried within three days.

Vertus said he wanted to experience death in as much of a Biblical fashion as possible, imitating Christ who was such a force in his life. He asked my pledge to ensure his wishes were honored. I assumed complete cooperation from the mortuary and with that, I gave him my word.

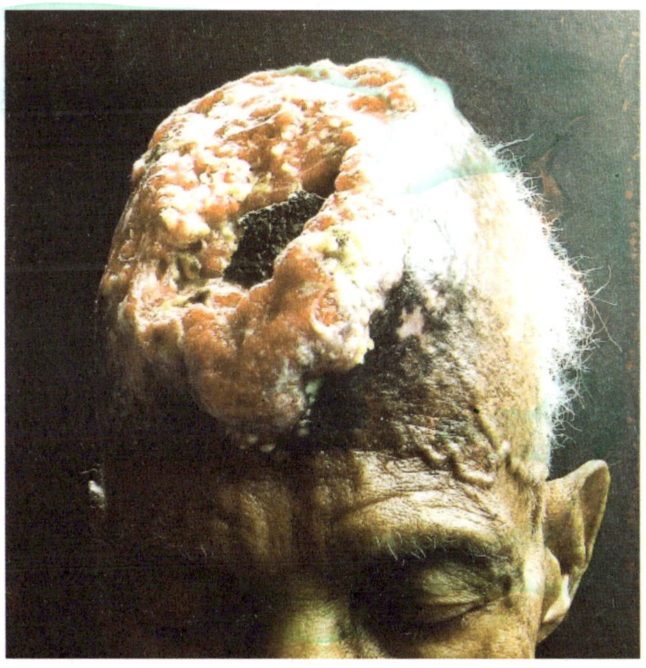

Vertus' forehead is drooping because of its detachment from his upper-scalp. The skull bone is exposed in the area, while a major portion of his skull has collapsed. To look inside Vertus' skull was quite sobering, but so was his heart.

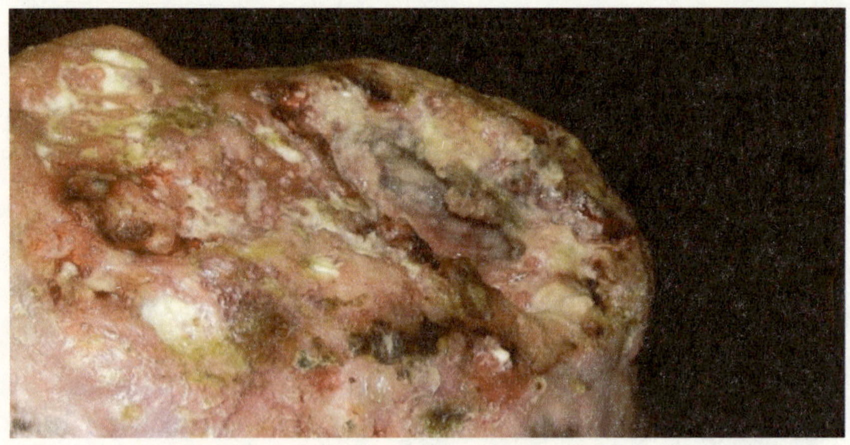

Above is a side view of Vertus' scalp as he faces the right side of this page.

His Night

Church leaders knew Vertus had become very ill and in turn wanted to do something special for him. In preparation for a happier occasion, the church decided to throw him the biggest celebration ever. It was Vertus who was usually there for others over the years, and now, it was his turn. The congregation would respond with a special banquet in his honor.

The planned celebration would say thank you, while at the same time wishing him a happy eighty-fifth birthday. A church member since the 1950s, the celebration dinner and program would involve about 300 guests. It was held in the church annex, a building about the size of a gymnasium.

I was not certain Vertus would be healthy enough to attend. Earlier that week, I was preparing for bed when my telephone rang. It was Vertus stating he was badly constipated. I was unaware of this and wondered why he had not mentioned it earlier. He placed his faith in over-the-counter medications that apparently were not working. I suggested that we conference with the 24-hour medical advice nurse, a service offered by his healthcare provider.

Vertus could hardly respond to the nurse due to his discomfort. She urged us to visit the local ER. When I heard this, I thought about my full schedule planned the following morning, beginning with breakfast at 7 am. Sitting in an emergency room ranked just above watching paint dry, but I grabbed my laptop and a magazine and headed for Vertus' house in anticipation of a long sleepless night. While in route, Vertus said, "Wilbert I'm sorry to have you out because of my problems. I want you to know that I appreciate you."

Once at the hospital, Vertus was called and tests were ordered. This was around 3:30 am. Medical staff provided needed relief through an enema and catheter. The decision was reached to admit him to the hospital for continued observation. This was Wednesday, March 6, two days before his big birthday celebration. I was very worried, not certain he would heal in time.

The next day I received a call from the event chair asking that I share heartening words about Vertus. Of course, I was delighted and saw this as my opportunity to extend well-deserved praise. Part of me wanted to tell his true story, while the other side knew that disclosing his secret was against his wishes. Too much information would hasten requests for him to show his wound. Vertus did not want that under any circumstances, the cost was simply too high.

I knew so much and was certain I knew Vertus better than anyone. I knew such trivia as the history of each of the wigs he owned over his lifetime. I could describe the styles he selected for them and the year he purchased each one. But I was handcuffed by his appeal not to have any public display surrounding his condition.

While preparing for the presentation, I pondered about what Vertus really meant when he said "No public display." I know he wanted no funeral, but these words would not be spoken at a funeral, this was a party, a celebration of his longevity and service. He always said that his funeral was preached by the way he lived. But no matter how I spun it, Vertus would be in attendance and I dare not risk hurting him, he meant the world to me.

Vertus was released from the hospital the following day and was at home resting. Friday morning I stopped in to check his status. He said, "I can barely stand but I want to be at my celebration." I suggested we use a wheelchair and he said we will have it there just in case. I knew he was making quite a sacrifice and I wasn't certain he could fulfill his intent. But he knew he was the star attraction and he didn't want to let anyone down.

I helped him choose his attire and stayed with him most of the day. He wore a black double-breasted suit with black shoes and chose a vibrant red shirt with a black western type choker. In place of his customary wool beanie, Vertus selected a black nylon fabric referred to by the now generation as a 'Wave Cap.' He would be sharply dressed for the occasion.

In professional basketball, a team fields five players and when the home team's crowd noise builds, it usually benefits the home team in a way that provides added excitement and subsequently makes them play harder. This home court advantage is referred to as the sixth man. It was as though the crowd at Vertus' party became that magical sixth man for him, providing him added energy and adrenalin. When the time arrived, Vertus was dressed and ready to go. This was his night staged in his house along with his church family.

Vertus received a hearty birthday wish, honored as a servant of God and humanity. Look closely to see the cover sponges hidden by the head covering. No one ever knew what was under the head cover.

Seated at the head table were the church pastor, politicians and key organizers. During the program politicians issued proclamations while some reminisced as far back as their teen years, when Vertus challenged them to obtain their college degree. It was a bittersweet night for me because Vertus made me think about my father, whom I missed, and now Vertus, whom I was certain would soon join him.

Finally I was introduced to deliver a tribute to Vertus. I hadn't prepared a script and must admit had no idea what I would say. As I took the walk forward I was very calm because I really knew Vertus. I looked his way before speaking and noticed his delicate smile. I knew at that moment he was proud of me and maybe in his own way, he also looked up to me. I was so happy because the feeling was mutual in every respect.

I began by acknowledging how pleased I was to lend my name to the long list of those whose life had been illuminated by Vertus. I reminded them that he courageously accepted the hand he was dealt, masterfully constructing a full house. I told them that Vertus did what every man aspires to do, he did his best and reminded them of the courage he has shown since an unfortunate day in 1927.

I alluded to the following; "If you only saw the challenge that existed under that beanie (I gestured towards Vertus), many of you would recoil at the sight." I continued, "And if you were forced to live life alongside the haunting voice of a lone medical technician, who eighty years ago shouted, 'Oh my God, I've given him too much,' you would have a different appreciation for all the things God has blessed you with."

I created questions in the minds of the audience, while purposely answering only a few of them. I hoped to leave them with a thirst for specifics that never arrived. They played along and accepted the confusion. They would not shower Vertus with sorrow and the best way to ensure that was to avoid disclosure of the problem. I did my part but in my heart I wanted them to know the full story. It was now time to hear from the honoree, introduced to an enthusiastic standing ovation.

Vertus began speaking before completely standing, "The worst thing about getting old is getting old." The audience chuckled before silence quickly befell the room. Vertus then in a very serious mood expressed appreciation and fondness for those present, those he called his extended family. He voiced the honor felt at being recognized. At that point he began to cry and when he did, it was contagious. He thanked everyone in his own way and tried equally hard to say goodbye! I knew in my heart that beneath the merriment of the celebration was sadness that he was seeing his church family maybe for the final time.

I remember the statement he made, "Tonight is a precursor to my trip to heaven." I believe it was his way of reminding us that there would be no further celebration or public display on his behalf. He stated that non-believers might classify him as just extraordinarily lucky, but he believed he was left here for 85 years for a higher purpose. He cautioned us to look for reasons to love. He gave the example of how difficult it is for some of us to forgive something as simple as a misunderstanding.

I saw tears everywhere, and white tissues sprouted as though they were budding gardenias in the spring. The audience knew Vertus was saying goodbye to them. Some told me later that they were caught by surprise and wanted to know what was wrong with Vertus. I told them that answer must come from him alone.

He concluded by stating publicly that he had forgiven those that in 1927 hurt a young boy. Maybe finally he was completely free and on top of his world, in that room, that night, and at that very moment. That day was Friday, March 9, 2007. Happy Birthday, Vertus!

Fellow choir member Dee Washington wishes Vertus her best, as she thanked him for their long friendship. Dee was a little girl when in the early 1960s she first met the man she always referred to as Mr. Hardiman. (Photo 2007)

Longtime tenant Gina Timbrello shared congratulatory wishes. Vertus glittered on the exterior but internally his health was quickly failing him. Neither Gina nor anyone else at the celebration knew what he hid under his beanie.

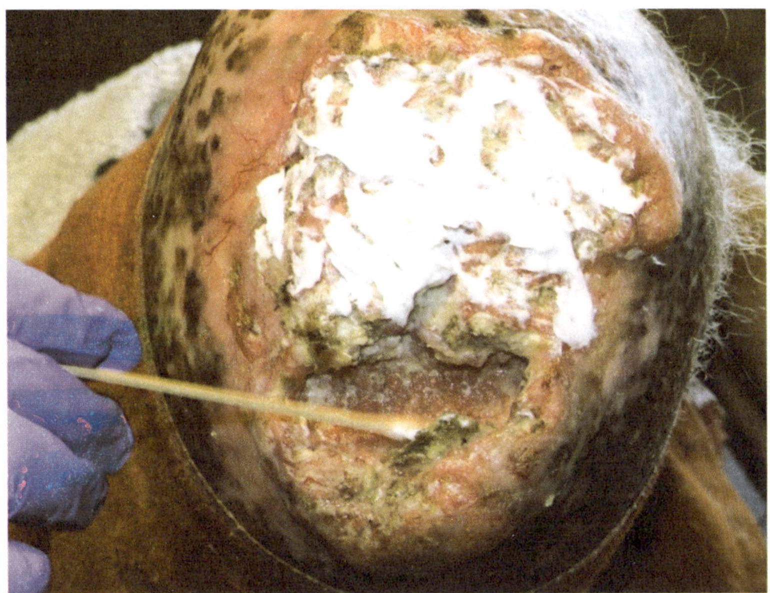

Incredibly this is what he hid. This photo was taken just two days following his birthday celebration during cleansing. There is a tile draped around Vertus' head as I applied medical cream. I thought long and hard about whether or not to include this photo, however, Vertus helped me. He wanted his memory to exist free from ever again hiding from others. He said, "I deserve to be accepted for who I am."

"It's not your place to judge me...but whatever you decide to do, remember somebody bigger than you and I always knows best."

-Vertus

FOLDING HIS TENT

Within weeks Vertus needed assistance with almost everything. The cancer was advancing and he was getting weaker. We moved him into the first floor condo that he purchased earlier that year. There was added sorrow when Vera called him stating their brother Melvin had just died from cancer. Since I began this journey, both Melvin and Fuzz were now gone and only three of the remaining ten victims were alive, Gletus, Horace and Vertus.

Remembering Melvin, I revisited portions of taped interviews I conducted with him. He spoke proudly about forgiveness, and said, "I just learned to live with it (his condition) and do the best I could. I don't feel any bitterness and I forgive whoever did this to me. It's something that happened and there's nothing we can do about it. I let go of thc past." Melvin had the distinction of being the second oldest member of his church. He was a rare example, who like Vertus was a church workaholic. He served as church treasurer, trustee, and Sunday school teacher while singing in the men's chorus.

Vertus began thinking of those he wanted to say goodbye to and his family doctor was one of them. I believed he just wanted to thank him. So we planned a trip to the clinic and arranged to meet with Dr. Waldron who sadly told Vertus, "There is nothing left that could improve your condition. You realize the end is near." Vertus looked him in the eye and nodded in confirmation. He did not ask how long he had to live and the doctor did not tell him so. The passion and tenderness I heard in the doctor's voice translated into the loss of my dear friend.

Dr. Waldron felt it was time to introduce Vertus to Hospice Care, a nonprofit organization referred to patients when they are terminally ill and death is expected within six months. On the way home Vertus told me, "I guess no matter how strong my religious beliefs, I'm still afraid of dying." At that point no matter what I said, I recognized Vertus was alone, the only thinker in his mind. It was he alone preparing to travel with only the Word of God to guide his way.

But for Vertus it was a moment to reflect. During general conversation he responded, "I showed them, didn't I? All those odds stacked against me for so many years." He reminded me of the words spoken by the reconstructive surgeon who was astonished at the then smaller toothpick sized hole in Vertus' head. He said, "I've seen individuals with a hole in their skull but they were not walking." The specialist was describing a cadaver within a morgue.

Word circulated that Vertus was now bedridden. Hospice sent representatives to visit him, with a view towards evaluating needed care and other essential supplies. They delivered a hospital bed among other things and scheduled a nurse by the name of Helen Brown. She was pleasant, and within minutes of arriving, I determined she was experienced and very good for Vertus.

Helen was not the least bit intimidated by the hole in Vertus' head. She never flinched at its sight, which I'm certain was emotionally pleasing for Vertus. Helen would prove to be a valued addition to Vertus' care team. I shared with her that when I took Vertus to visit his doctors, he was assumed to be in the worst imaginable pain and subsequently was prescribed the ultimate, most powerful drugs.

The worst, and most powerful drug was now Fentanyl, an opiate derivative that is many times stronger than morphine. Nicknamed the dying man's drug, it's used primarily to treat terminally ill cancer patients. Once prescribed there is generally no turning back from its addiction. The power of the drug causes deep sleep, leaving little desire to eat, speak or even think. I appealed to Helen to contact Vertus' doctor to reduce dosages; my request was granted.

There was also the constant task of flushing the wound, a chore I now shared with Helen. We both spoke with positive words to Vertus, confirming that he appeared better, a response that affected him therapeutically. I read publications provided by Hospice to better understand the dying process. These perspectives were helpful, though nothing could make the pain I felt from Vertus' death go away.

At week's end, I went to Karaoke and heard a song about dreamers seeking to arrive at another place in life. The task to get back to the past was difficult, but all along the dreamer had the God given power to make it happen. Judy Garland originally performed the song *Somewhere Over The Rainbow* in the tale, *The Wizard of Oz*. When compared, the song has much to say about the victims from Lyles Station.

Possibly somewhere up high, where the skies are a lovelier shade of blue, Vertus will exist without fear of further scorn or ridicule. And even if Vertus found it difficult to cosmetically fit in on earth, because he had the faith to trust and follow bluebirds, they will guide him to a powerful embrace awaiting him in the beyond.

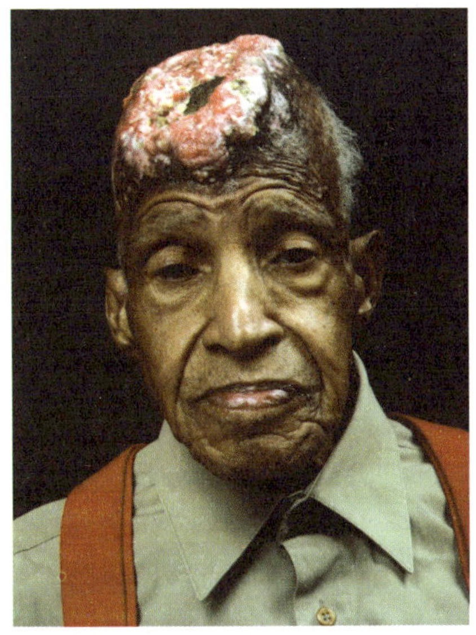

Vertus' cancer was well within its final stage. This view shows Vertus, the face of a very tired man.

"Maybe the technician wanted the opportunity to tell me and the other victims how wrong the experiments were and how sorry she was to be a part of them."

-Vertus

A Setting Sun

In the days that followed, well-wishers sent flowers and cards. I read some of them to Vertus, some more than once. At this stage, it was good for him to feel loved; however, he was so sick and too heavily sedated to fully comprehend. He slept soundly for hours, many times on an empty stomach diminishing his strength to fight the cancer. I guess he was working in concert with the Creator, both handling things their way. I knew the time had arrived to avoid interference. I no longer attempted to encourage him to eat or drink. I got it. I simply accepted reality.

I understood the price Vertus paid to survive and knew just how long he paid it. It was a life-long struggle, and maybe the Creator felt it high time he's allowed to hoist a white flag and come on home. I believe that was the way Vertus saw it. I was so sad, yet so happy for him at the same time. It was so easy to cry for both emotions.

Vertus often said, "Some of us worry so much about what we need God to do for us that we forget what God has already done over our lives." Vertus never forgot, always first thanking God for allowing him to live long enough to share his story. He made it clear, "The Lord did not have to let me live this long."

I found comfort in literature produced by Hospice. Before now, I had no real interest in the subject of death and I'm certain if not for Vertus, I would not have been the wiser. One publication was entitled *The Stages of Grief*, authored by Dr. Ross. She wrote about death and dissected grief into five stages.

I found interest in these stages and learned that each one must be traveled before real healing could begin. The stages were denial, anger, bargaining, letting go and acceptance. I stepped inside each stage to determine which one I was facing, although I eventually realized I was experiencing stage four and five, letting go and acceptance. It was made clear that these stages didn't necessarily occur in any particular order.

LETTING GO

She called letting go the beginning of the end. When bargaining failed, I would realize that Vertus had gone and I would learn to let go of him. She added that it would not be easy but must be done in my own time. It could take weeks, months or even years but eventually I would come to realize that Vertus is really gone and will never come back.

ACCEPTANCE

Acceptance is when I realize that this is final and that life must go on without Vertus. I will accept it as it was meant to be, a path through life that must be journeyed. Though I would always love and miss Vertus, I would realize that I am alive and must go on living my life without him.

Hospice also taught me that Vertus would lose interest in most things and he was clearly doing that. He may want to reminisce for extended periods of time about both joys and sorrows. I was encouraged to take time to listen to what was important to him, and that he will continue to sleep soundly both day and night. These points were very familiar to me.

Other thoughts warned that Vertus would shut down naturally and would eventually require and want less food. At that point it was suggested I offer him sips of fluids, using a flexible straw as long as he could comfortably swallow. If he reaches the point he is unable to swallow, it suggested I offer him bits of ice chips. And finally it urged me to keep his lips moist with lip balm and his mouth clean with a soft damp cloth.

When I entered Vertus' room, I made certain he felt my presence though he was seemingly asleep. Today I made sure he received a dose of his favorite gospel music. He adored songs by Mahalia Jackson and Kenneth Glover, two of his favorite artists. I usually had old time gospel playing softly by his bedside. I once asked him, "Which rhythm and blues artist came to mind as a favorite?" He could not think of a single one. He replied, "They didn't do anything for me, I was always partial to gospel music."

Helen from Hospice was also there. She too became attached to Vertus, though in her business she tried to keep a professional distance. But, after learning about the experiments, she was captivated.

It was becoming clear that the spirits uniting my dad and Vertus were stronger than ever. Though the men had never met, the traumas associated with their heads were by now interwoven into a single event. Perhaps I was developing closure, saying goodbye to my dad by way of Vertus, clinging to a thread hanging from a garment called life. There was little time remaining to know my dad better and to have a chance to finally tell him how much I loved him and hoped he was resting in eternal peace. I now felt so much closer to him through Vertus. In fact, when I held Vertus' hand I was also holding my father's hand in mine. It was now so clear to me.

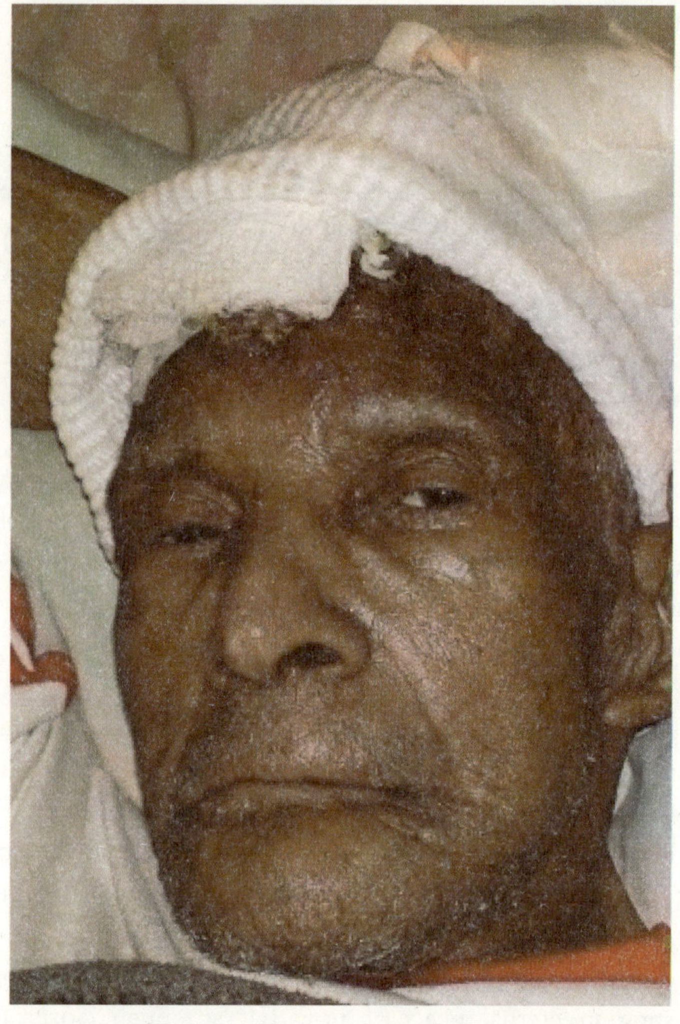

When I awakened Vertus, he had no idea whether it was day or night. He told me about a trip he had just concluded to Indiana. He said his mother Irene asked him to say hello and thanked me for being a part of his life. Of course none of this occurred but I knew it was important to agree with him. In his mind's eye, these events were as real as one could imagine. (Photo 2007)

A Prayer for Him

I attended church and informed the pastor of Vertus' end of life status and sought permission to make a general announcement. The minister chose to share the message himself. There were about three hundred in attendance. During the announcement the church was quiet and still.

It was sobering as the pastor told of Vertus' turn for the worst and subsequently urged each of us to pray for him. There seemed to be an extraordinary spirit in the air. I'm certain we worshiped knowing that if he were able, Vertus would be singing in our midst, wearing that familiar smile while swaying in the choir rhythmically off key, yet very happy.

Many remembered that I was telling his story and made it a point to communicate their sorrows. They shared the positive influences Vertus had on their lives. Some of the more senior members reminded me of his decades of devoted service. It was always the old stories that seemed to fascinate me. Whether it was someone in need that he granted a loan, a member of a family without food, or a troubled soul who simply needing a friend, I heard them all; Vertus was a celebrity.

This information came to me not only at church, but in the market, post office and bank to name a few. And with respect to his status, there was always the question, "How's he doing?" My response was an honest one, "His time is short. Life here on earth is drawing to a close." I guess as it relates to death, most find the conversation uncomfortable, though death is always the final chapter in every life.

I went to Vertus' house about midday to clean and dress the hole in his head. Vertus slept through the entire process. I touched him frequently to remind him I was present. He held my hand a time or two, even while sleeping. I recall periods when my hand was numb but any attempt to remove it would awaken Vertus. His breathing patterns were distressed. I knew that my friend was very close to his fall into the arms of angels seated at his bedside.

Perhaps just as he so strongly believed, these angels would take him to a throne of judgment where the Lord would welcome him and recognize the admirable path he traveled. Vertus believed this and chose to live his life in accordance to the Lord's commandments, ultimately rewarded by these words at journey's end…"Job well done." These were the kinds of things Vertus shared to all that cared to listen.

The following Sunday morning I was singing in the choir and while warming up in the choral room, in lieu of our traditional prayer circle, we sang the gospel song entitled *Soon As I Get Home.* We each recognized this song as one of Vertus' favorites, perhaps because it spoke volumes of the relief Vertus so profoundly sought. It was the carrot that motivated him to carry on during times most would have given up. Before we began to sing, I asked that we sing it for Vertus. The song's lyrics describe how one day, when it is all over, we will have a new robe and crown to wear.

I shed tears for Vertus that morning. I realized that I had come full circle in my friendship with him. During that time, twenty years had passed since I first stood in fellowship with him. I now stood alone, truly missing and praying for my best friend and surrogate father. I thanked God for the impact Vertus had on my life. It would be a few more days before I realized that when it came to this story, a three-leg stool had been formed and like most stools, it could not stand without the presence of all three legs.

A LULLABY

Today was very difficult, while at the same time peaceful. During my visit I noticed his extremities, particularly the hands and feet felt cold. My first inclination was to add a blanket or two until Helen advised me that at a time such as this, it was the body's natural reaction to slow its blood flow from the heart. Subsequently, the furthest extremities, Vertus' hands and feet, would normally become discolored and cool. He was much smaller now, estimated to weigh about 80 pounds. He was feeble, attempting to steady himself in the gravity of what little life remained.

I sat and wondered about the varying degrees in which we cope with death, realizing that some deal with it daily, as first responders to keep us alive. Some wonder how anyone could live this way. I was asked a similar question when it came to caring for Vertus and the hole in his head. For me, a conversion occurred the moment he shared his hunger to be simply seen as any human being. He didn't ask anything special but was a special man able to take a small piece of this world and live in it as best he could. This he accomplished while ignoring those willing to make him the subject of cruel jokes and disparagement.

I assumed that for those of us who knew and loved him, Vertus was very normal, and we granted him the acceptance he so longed for. And in his final chapter, we fulfilled his wish for the same dignified walk destined for us all. I knew that I deserved no better fate than he, and possessed no greater value merely because I was fortunate enough **not** to be the subject of a boyhood experiment.

I was relieved because now I understood that what was done to Vertus in 1927 hurt him, but what occurred following that day, inflicting not physical pain but equally destructive emotional pain, perhaps hurt him even greater. As I remembered back toward the beginning of my relationship with Vertus, I realized the selfishness of my attempts to 'help' him improve his looks. My early criticisms were trivial. It was clear to me during this moment that the incredible path of discovery led me to a better understanding—an understanding that changed my life forever. I have released the guilt I felt and have found a way to forgive even myself.

I thought to call Vertus' sister Vera to let her know that Vertus was near death; the signs became increasingly glaring. Nothing seemed capable of reversing this inevitable outcome. I didn't look forward to the conversation because just weeks earlier, Vera had to say goodbye to their brother Melvin.

The following morning, I went to the office. It was difficult to focus. Each time the telephone rang, I was afraid it was Helen calling to tell me Vertus was gone. I was certain he would die at any moment. By lunchtime, I was so filled with anxiety I had only one real option. I left the office and walked the two blocks to his home. As usual, I had my camera with me. I was committed to capture his life until the very end.

One of Vertus' last requests was for me to play the classical song entitled *Somewhere In Time* as close to the very end as possible. Vertus always found that song so soothing and beautiful and at times would play it for hours. I knew it was time to honor his request, and I felt so proud that he was living out this chapter according to his wishes. I interrupted the gospel songs playing at his bedside and for the final time, dialed up this selection played just for him. I placed the CD player on repeat mode and selected the song to escort him from this earth. It is one of the many ways I will always be reminded of him.

I wasn't certain he could comprehend the moment. As I played the song I felt for him a profound peace and tranquility. I could smell the fresh roses purchased from the flower shop located between my office and his home, a stop I so willingly made.

Most of Vertus' friends and acquaintances chose to say their goodbye at the birthday celebration. When the telephone rang, it was usually someone asking how he was resting. The response was always, resting comfortably. In his room were sounds of the respiratory equipment producing and propelling oxygen into his frail body. There were no options for a feeding tube due to other complications that might ensue. Vertus made it clear that we were not to attempt anything designed to prolong his dying.

Vertus had just received a final bit of nourishment in the form of a simple chip of ice; his weight by now was approximately 75 pounds.

"I know who I am and whose I am."

-Vertus

A LONG GOODNIGHT

At this point he was unable to swallow. The muscles in his neck would not respond. Even feeble attempts to swallow simple drops of water were causing severe choking. I sat by his bedside and wrote: "I know I will never hear my friend Vertus ever speak to me again. It is now that I must rely on his past words to forever shape the memories I am destined to hold forever, memories of a man I along with many others, have come to love." Vertus received his final ice chip at 5:35 p.m. on Wednesday, May 30, 2007. From that point on, Vertus clung to the little life that remained.

It was Friday, June 1, when Helen and I arrived at Vertus' bedside almost simultaneously. Her first task was to evaluate his meds, pulse and overall condition. She changed his medical patch and began to share with me the reality of her job. Of course, working for Hospice, Helen cares for terminally ill patients, and she reminded me what that meant...with time, she loses 100% of them.

Once she completed her approximate hour-long task, I was heading to my office with plans to return later. I routinely stated that I would see her another day. At this point she replied, "I don't think Vertus will last another day! Wilbert, this will more than likely be the last time I see you. I wish you well."

She added that she had seen thousands during their final hours and was certain Vertus was exhibiting life-ending characteristics. I believed Helen and treated this day as if it were his last. I decided to stay longer. All I could think of was how much I had yet to say. I communicated with Vertus the entire time, though he was not coherent. I wanted him to know I was here with him as I promised, here to the very end. I then held his hand and told him I loved him.

I used this time to share my sentiments about the journey Vertus started in my life. Though he was on his deathbed, I sensed both he and my father were present. I spoke freely in conversation, sensing all three of us were present in that room. I took the opportunity to thank him for the extraordinary impact he made on my life. I also said goodbye to my biological father, since I never had the chance to do so when he passed. Symbolically, I was not merely holding a single hand but instead united were the hands of all three of us, perhaps each sharing a respect and special love for the other.

I immediately began sharing long held urgencies and longings for a father. And I wanted this understood while the men were still metaphorically present for a short while longer. They were leaving together, both carried by the same band of angels.

I continued talking while I still had the chance. I told the men that I had not complained about a single health condition since the first day Vertus shared the story of the experiments. And if not compelling enough, I realized I would never again complain, because no matter how difficult I believed my condition was, there was those worst off than me, each willing to trade places.

If I could speak with my dad one final time, I would say, "Dad, this life lesson was entrenched when I recalled your horrifying fate. At a special moment a unique transposition began, forever linking you and Vertus. This union created something very special. Dad, I will never forget your undeserved fate as you laid helpless, your precious head swelled to twice its normal size. I believe that the person who swung the instrument of death, if not already, will one day give account for their actions."

I talked with them about my newfound appreciation for writing, researching and storytelling. I told of my gift to forgive others and how my life is richer because I shed the baggage of past deeds weighing me down. It was my hope that they better understood the imprint they made on my life and how it has left me a better person. There were profound lessons associated with alcohol abuse and child abandonment, the fact that I will never engage in either because of the firsthand destruction I experienced as a child.

And yes, I reminisced on the fun times through my recollection of a funny story. I chuckled at one of Vertus' familiar quotes; "If I tell you a rooster dips snuff, look under his wing for the can." This was Vertus' comical way of suggesting that I follow his instruction without question. And his saying, "Don't allow the devil to ride, because if you let him ride he will very soon want to drive."

And the reminder of the poetic passage that kept Vertus grounded particularly during life's difficult moments that went as follows: *I used to cry and sing the blues, for on my feet I had no shoes, until I met upon the street, an orphan child who had no feet. Be thankful, there is someone worst off than you—be grateful, there are those who would love to be in your shoes.* I'm not certain of the poem's author but Vertus sure found comfort in its message.

But when I searched for similar moments with you dad, the single thing that comes to mind is your smile. Perhaps the lessons you taught me in word along with the 33 years since your passing has taken its toll.

There was no more Karaoke for a while. Instead, I thought of a song written and performed by Smokey Robinson at the gravesite of longtime member of the singing Temptations, Melvin Franklin. The song entitled *Really Gonna Miss You* has lyrics describing how I felt.

> *Really Gonna Miss You*
> *It's really gonna be different without you*
> *Time is gonna be hard and slow*

For the rest of my life
Gonna be thinking about you
Time came when you had to go

I'll miss you my buddy
I'll miss you my friend
I promise my love for you, will never end

In your finest hour
I was there with you
And without you
Things won't be the same

But there's a higher power
That we answer to
And you heard him calling your name

Really gonna miss you
Everything about you
Your smiling face
I know you want us all to be strong

Really gonna miss you
But I know you're going
To that magic place
Singing you a brand new song

I'll miss you my buddy, I'll miss you my friend
I promise my love for you, Will never end

While seated at Vertus' bedside, I saw a life loaded with strange twist and turns. I would find it hard to imagine suffering the effects of a violent experiment conducted by a hospital, then to ironically enter a hospital daily for over forty years as a manager and leader for others.

I'm not certain I could have so easily done that. It would have been so difficult to avoid the bad memories I so longed to forget.

Vertus died Friday, June 1, 2007, at 8:22 pm. I wanted to cry but had no tears. I instead found happy thoughts of his final peace and took comfort in the fact that the hole in his head and subsequent cancer was not caused by something he did or failed to do.

I lowered his bed to lay him flat before he became inflexible. I next opened his Bible reciting Psalm 23 as he previously requested within moments of his death. I spoke the scripture with a sense of pride and eager enthusiasm. Following the scripture reading, I knew Vertus was at peace; God wanted him now. He left just as he was, leaving behind the wig and beanie along with those he hid from. They were no longer requirements for him to achieve happiness. It was his heart that was important now and his legacy of great servitude.

I called Vera and Uncle Gletus who reacted with words of sorrow. They lingered on the telephone as though I was their final link to Vertus. Uncle Gletus commented, "That boy suffered." I responded, "You are right." But I also reminded him that Vertus forgave those who in 1927 did this to him. They asked about funeral arrangements and wanted to be notified when they were complete. This was awkward because of Vertus' instruction to have no public display.

My next call was for Helen who assumed that Vertus was gone. She was correct. She was at her residence and took time to make a point of her sadness and sorrow. She identified him as a favorite patient and concluded with a pledge to arrive in approximately thirty minutes.

Her job was to verify death and complete official records required by state and local authorities. I proceeded to notify the mortuary who simultaneously radio dispatched the body transport company. I heard them give Vertus' name and address along with other relevant facts described in rather official terms. They detailed his ethnicity, height and approximate weight. I heard them assign a case number. I confirmed the address for pick-up and gave my name as the contact person. They estimated 1 to 1 ½ hours before arrival, a promise broken numerous times over before finally arriving at 1:27 am.

In the meantime, Helen was completing mounds of paperwork. Since a doctor examined Vertus within the past 25 days, the coroner was not involved. It was verified by Hospice that death was not at the hands of another. Helen was busy counting the unused medications, placing them in hot soapy water inside a container made for just such purposes. She had walked this road countless times and was regimented in her actions.

Once she left, the hours began to tick ever so slowly. The room was motionless and Vertus lay there so peacefully. I sat by his side and noticed the strangest phenomena. I continued to hear the breathing apparatus for hours after it was shut off as though still feeling the motion of a boat ride long after walking ashore. When I looked at Vertus I momentarily saw his chest expand. I surmise it was my mind playing tricks on me because I never saw his chest lying still, void of any motion. I'm sure I saw the illusion I wanted to see.

A vintage clock resting on the nightstand continued to tick noticeably contrasting a room completely filled with silence. The time was approaching 11 pm. I again telephoned the mortuary that responded with an updated expected time of arrival. I took the delay in stride, imagining that they seldom receive a complaint for their tardiness, due to the fact they are removing a loved one we are so often reluctant to let go. I knew Vertus was with me for the last time, and I really did not want to rush our final parting.

Finally two men entered, in their mid to late twenties. One

concentrated on completing necessary paperwork while the other diligently prepared Vertus for transport. The preparation was conducted in a unique way, synonymous with the ceremonial folding of the American flag. The wrapping of Vertus in the white sheet, the related folding and expert draping and tucking of its ends. Every roll of his body was systematic, making the overall display one of dignity and care. I asked one of the men to estimate Vertus' weight and they thought 75 to 80 pounds.

The gurney was left at the front door. As they went to retrieve it, I asked them to wait. I explained that I wished to carry Vertus out of his home, through the front door. I wanted to place him on the awaiting gurney. I didn't wait for their reply. I concurrently lifted Vertus and carried him as though he were a bouquet of roses shaped in the form of his frail body. I placed Vertus on the gurney and began walking alongside his body with my hand cradling his head. I suspected he was already wearing his new crown.

"I don't feel anger and I forgive those who did this to me."

-Vertus

A LESSON REMAINS

It was then that I realized how deeply I would miss my buddy, as much as I miss my father. How did this simple man take me on such a journey? Most of us will never do great things, but we each can do small things in a big way.

Through the eyes of Vertus Hardiman at last I can see. I know now that his lifelong problem was not with the world. The real problem is instead with others. And for all those times I was blind, I never realized it was the harsh judgment of people, like you, and me, that caused him such pain.

When we criticize and pass judgment on another, we take upon ourselves the awesome responsibility of rightness. After all, the wrong judgment comes with a high price, all too often paid by the very person who is wrongly judged. Naturally, all things invite judgment—the weather, the taste of food or a television program. Each day, something invites us to judge it.

Willingly, we render our judgments without thinking about the consequences of our actions. We judge, and then to make matters more complex, we believe in our judgment. Perhaps what we fail to realize, is that our judgment has the power to impose suffering on both the accused and each of us.

From the time Vertus entered my office and shared his secret with me, I wanted to forever look for the beauty in my fellow man, and never measure anyone's worth by the way they may look. For it is what is underneath the exterior that carries the greatest weight. And under no circumstances will I endeavor to complain, for when I feel the urge, I will first think of Vertus.

I want to possess the capacity to see my blessings. Is this not what the Creator calls us to do? What will you do to make life easier for an unsuspecting victim of an unfortunate tragedy, that next Vertus Hardiman that enters your life?

Vertus left me comfort and assurance in my belief that he dwells in the presence of the ultimate caretaker, the one who guarantees he will never be frowned upon or ever harmed again. Farewell my dear friend…for your memory shall journey with me forever.

As I wrote these words, I started crying as I have so many times. But this time I could not stop my tears for it was not until now, years following Vertus' death, that I buried him. He accompanied me in spirit as I told his story.

I reflected upon the incredible life of my friend at the Karaoke Lounge while listening to a song entitled *At Last,* made famous by Etta James. As Cynthia sang, I felt the power contained in the words, *At Last,* though to many in the audience, it perhaps had little meaning. For me, it embodied Vertus' longings for so many years.

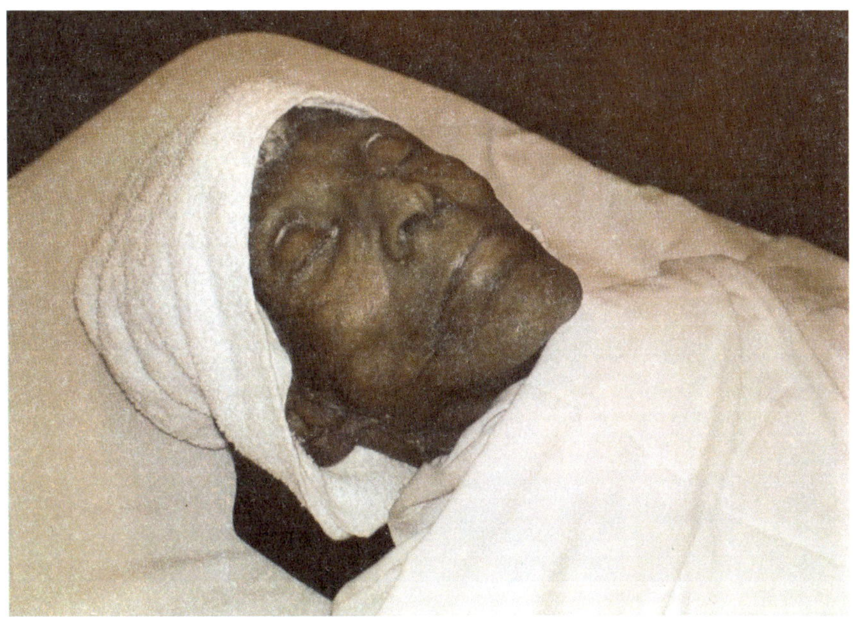

Vertus closed his eyes and went to sleep. Now it is his Creator who holds and comforts him. Vertus many times had told me, "I know who I am and whose I am."

"I have suffered a lot of pain and I am tired of carrying this burden."

-Vertus

EPILOGUE

The two surviving victims of the Lyles experiments are Gletus Hardiman of Lyles Station and Horace Hardiman of Indianapolis, Indiana. To date none whom I met ever remembered a consoling thought or anyone offering an apology for the experiments. Some residents of Lyles Station still today are unable to think of the hospital as a place committed to improve and prolong life. For them it is forever a place of misfortune.

At the time of death, Vertus had a net worth of eight million dollars. He left 75% of that wealth to his church and the remaining 25% to his favorite charity. Both gifts at the time were considered one of the largest ever granted.

I hope after reading this book you know Vertus almost as well as I. It is my wish that you realize that when we have no shoes, there are things of far greater importance, because just around the corner is a Vertus Hardiman, who has no feet. During times of adversity, I hope you choose not to react with anger, but, instead, pause to weigh the consequences. Then remember Vertus, the man who chose to forgive.

Vertus' death brought such sadness but most certainly he would want us to share his joy as he entered into his "New home." It is comforting to know that he will never again be seen as an "Elephant Man," instead he will be recognized as beautiful and spectacular as any other in heaven.

When I come to the end of the road,
And the sun has set for me,
I want no rites in a gloom filled room,
Why cry for a soul set free

Miss me a little, but not too long,
And not with your head bowed low,
Remember the love that we once shared,
Miss me - but let me go

For this is a journey we must all take,
And each must go along,
It's all part of the "Master's" plan,
A step on the road to home

When you are lonely and sick at heart,
Go to the friends we know,
And bury your sorrows in doing good deeds,
Miss me - but let me go.

~ Author Unknown ~

My buddy, Vertus Welborn Hardiman
Born March 9, 1921
Died June 1, 2007

THE END

The Lyles Station 10

Melvin LaDon Hardiman
2/9/1921-4/28/2007

Ella Mae Hardiman-Green
3/26/1917-3/5/1998

Horace M. Hardiman
Born 11/28/1919

Vertus W. Hardiman
3/9/1922-6/1/2007

Milburn Stewart
6/19/1917-4/17/1991

Gletus R. Hardiman
Born 10/2/1920

Garwood V. Hardiman
6/20/1916-2/08/2002

Melvin (Fuzz) Hardiman
6/8/1920-1/1/2007

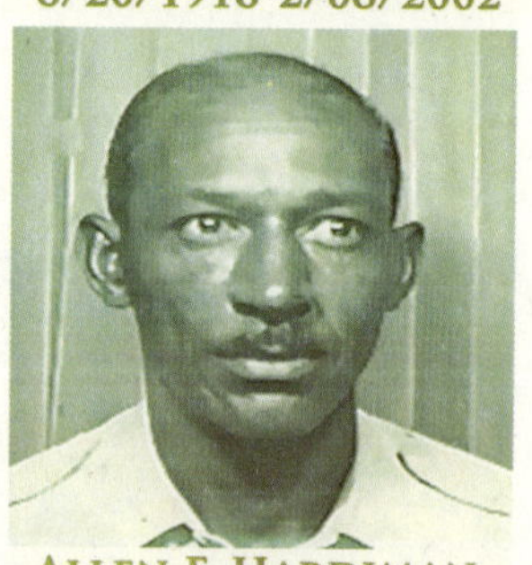

Allen F. Hardiman
4/12/1921-4/16/1986

Lloyd Hardiman
8/31/1921-6/14/1944

Questions for Use by Educators

Self-Worth

1. When you hurt inside, does it make you feel the need to hurt someone else? Does misery really love company?

2. Can you make yourself feel better, by pushing down another for whatever reason?

3. Does criticizing another make you feel more important and better than what you really are?

4. When you are feeling hurt, what is your first reaction? What is the best thing to do?

5. In what ways can a person elevate his or her own self-worth? Is this important?

6. Do you know where to go for help when a situation is too hard for you to handle on your own? Who would you go to for help and why?

Relationships and Communication

1. Why do people hurt other people's feelings, even though they know it is not the right thing to do?

2. Would you tease another person if you knew it could push them to the point of severely injuring themselves or, even worse, taking their own lives? (Explain)

3. What is hatred and how is it different from hurt?

4. Who do you hold a grudge against and why?
5. What are some reasons many give for postponing forgiveness?

6. When did you last forgive someone? In what way was it helpful for all concerned?

7. Have you ever lost someone very close to you? How did it affect your relationship with others? Did you react with anger? Did you withdraw?

8. Caregiving is a gift we give to others. Have you ever given care to someone? Was the experience rewarding or did you regret your need to give your time and energy?

BULLYING

1. When you see someone being picked on by a bully, what can you do to help?

2. What does a bully look like? Act like?

3. Do students have confidence that adults can, or will, do their best to protect them from harm? (Explain)

4. Have you thought about how your actions or words could hurt another's feelings? (Explain)

5. Could you be a bully and not know that you are? (Explain)

6. Are you aware that the suicide rate for high school students are very high and that many teens commit suicide as a result of bullying? How would you feel if someone you were mean to committed suicide?

7. What changes could you make in your life to be more sensitive to how your actions are hurting someone else?

8. Have you considered that just because another is different from you or has different beliefs, that it is not acceptable to make fun of them or say hurtful things? Why?

Questions For Use By Educators

Complete school curriculum, documentary film and other related items are available at:

www.upliftproductionsinc.com

The life of Vertus Hardiman shows us the way to love and not hate.

YOUR FRIEND FOREVER,

WILBERT L. SMITH PH.D.